A RUSHING MIGHTY WIND

Michael H. Francis

Paul enters Rome

A RUSHING MIGHTY WIND

Book Three of GOD'S HAND IN HISTORY

BY

MARY WILSON

Illustrated by Vera Louise Drysdale

OUR SUNDAY VISITOR, INC.
HUNTINGTON, INDIANA 46750

First published in 1963 by Blandford Press Ltd.

© 1977 Blandford Press Ltd.
Link House, West Street, Poole, Dorset

This edition published by arrangement with
Blandford Press Ltd.

ISBN: 0–87973–697–6
Library of Congress Catalog Card Number: 77–81933

Published in the U.S.A. by
Our Sunday Visitor, Inc.
Noll Plaza
Huntington, Indiana 46750

697

CONTENTS

Sign-post People

GOD'S ideas for the world are always a long way ahead of what most people are thinking and doing; so much so that the world never quite catches up with them.

But God sees to it that in every age there are one or more men and women who are ahead of their time and called by Him to point the way for humanity to follow. You might describe them as Sign-post People. You can see the next place written on them before you get there.

Many people come to a sign-post to find out which way to go. Ordinary men and women looking for the right way to go have to choose whether they will go their own way or God's way. They must all make their own decisions, but it may be a help in making up their minds to look at the lives of the Sign-post People who have gone on ahead, and draw their own conclusions.

Of course, there is always a time when the Sign-post person is neither on ahead nor in the past, but living in the world with us, and generally there are only a few who recognise the Sign-post People when they turn up. The rest have a way of turning against them and trying to destroy them. But looking back to their lives after they have died we see them more clearly.

We can also see the chances the world missed because not enough people followed the sign-post.

I hope these stories may help you to recognise Sign-post People when you come across them in the world today and not have to wait until they are dead.

6

The Promise

WE have now reached another turning point in history. In the earlier books we have followed God's Plan for the world, partly through great thinkers and philosophers of the east who devoted themselves to finding out what were the real and lasting things in life, and partly through the story of one family and nation whom God chose for a particular purpose.

This purpose was that it should be the family on earth to which He sent His Son, who would show all men how to live.

But because the world is a battleground between Good and Evil, in which everyone has to take sides, the coming of the Son of God made it very clear that there was no half-way house. People were either for Him or against Him once they had heard and understood what He had come to show.

He said that the world was made by God and was His world. That God was the Father of all men and that God alone knew how to run it.

He Himself had come to show the way to God which would bring sight and healing to all mankind. But men, then as now, wanted to run things in their way, and after a short time they turned on Jesus and killed Him.

But this was only the first round of a battle which is at its height in the world today. For though Jesus was put to death by people who wanted their own way, on the third day God brought Him back to life, and no one has ever been able to kill Him again.

He stayed with His friends on earth for a time, talking and eating with them.

This gave some of them the idea that after all He had come back to make the Jewish people great once more as they had been in the days of David and Solomon.

Here He was, alive and well again. Surely this was the moment to make up for all the seeming disgrace and defeat and show their enemies that their King was back with them.

'Will you now restore the Kingdom to Israel?' they asked impatiently.

But Jesus told them it was not for them to know more than God told them at any given time.

He said that He was soon going to return to God, His Father, but that after He had gone a new power would be let loose in the world which would be available for everyone ever after.

At the end of six weeks He called them all together on a hill just outside Jerusalem and said to them, 'Wait in the city of Jerusalem and when you have received this power, go and tell people about Me, not only in Jerusalem but in Judæa and Samaria and right to the ends of the earth.'

Then He was taken from their sight, and the men and women who had been with Him for three years were left, apparently alone.

As they stood gazing upwards, trying to follow Him with their eyes, they suddenly became aware of two men in white standing beside them, who said to them, 'Why are you standing looking up like that? One day Jesus will come back in the same way that you have seen Him go.'

This has not yet happened. Perhaps it will not happen till the world is more ready for it than it is now—or was then.

There was still a lot to do to prepare for it, so the little band of friends, about a hundred and twenty men and women, turned back to Jerusalem as they had been told. To this day we do not know who most of them were.

They were a hundred and twenty people just like any of us. They were alone. There was no one to back them or bail them out if they got into difficulties. They had nothing to go on except what Jesus had said to them, but it was enough.

So they all went back to Jerusalem to wait for the power which He had promised them.

This time it was not so much a Sign-post person as a Sign-post group.

They had chosen, as we have to choose, between a world run by God for His purposes and a world run by men for their purposes.

It would not lead to the rule of one nation over others, but to the rule of God over all nations. In the course of time each nation would find its place, not only free from the rule of its neighbours, but free from the hates and greeds and divisions which stop all freedom.

As they walked back to Jerusalem, we have no evidence that they knew this, or understood that their complete trust in Jesus and in each other was to lay the foundations of a new society.

New Power let loose in the world

THEY went back to the house where Jesus had eaten the Last Supper with the twelve men who had been with Him for the last three years of His time on earth. They were to wait there for the power He had promised. By that time there were only eleven left because Judas Iscariot, when he realised what he had done in betraying Jesus, went away and killed himself.

They decided to make the numbers up to twelve again, and from among those who had known and worked with Jesus, they chose a man called Matthias.

Then, together, they waited. They wanted nothing for themselves, and were all of one mind, in one place. There were no doubts or divisions among them to prevent the new power from coming.

They just prayed, and stayed together and waited, knowing that they could have absolute confidence in the promise Jesus had given them. It does not seem that the promise was fulfilled the same day, so they had to have both faith and patience.

They waited till the Jewish Feast of Pentecost. Then, says the man who wrote the account of these early days which we call the Acts of the Apostles, the Power came, like a rushing mighty wind. It filled all the houses where they were sitting, bringing light and warmth like flames of fire playing round the heads of all who were there.

It was a force stronger than electricity or atomic energy, the power to transform not just metals and atoms, but people's whole nature, so that these quite ordinary men and women were transformed into wholly different personalities.

This power was released in the world then, and has been here ever since, available for all who fulfil the conditions for receiving it, as those men and women did. It gave them new life and new courage, and they became the heart of a new society. They were ready to give all they had to make a new world, and because they gave everything, the new world began growing up around them.

The change in them was so startling that many of their friends thought they were drunk. But Peter, a very different Peter from the man who had run from Jesus the night He was arrested, explained what had happened.

'These men are not drunk,' he said. 'It's only midday. This is simply what was foretold by the prophet Joel when he said, "I will pour out

my spirit on your sons and daughters, and will show wonders in heaven and signs on earth".'

There were many more people than usual in Jerusalem at this time because of the Feast Day, and Jews had come to it from many other countries. Peter spoke forthrightly to the assembled multitude about their responsibility for the death of Jesus. They had killed Jesus, he said, a man approved by God. What they had done was an extremely serious matter, but Jesus had proved stronger than death, for He was both Lord and Christ.

He did not mince his words, but he said that they could be forgiven and make a fresh start if they were really sorry. Many of them did this. They took responsibility for where their nation had gone wrong, and three thousand people started a new life, determined to work together and enlist others.

And every day new people joined them.

Peter and John and the lame man

AMAZING things began to happen through these new men. They went daily to the Temple together to pray. One day as Peter and John went through what was known as 'The Beautiful Gate', they passed a lame man who was sitting begging.

This man had had something wrong with his feet ever since he was born, and had never been able to walk. As he could not earn his living, his friends carried him to the door of the Temple every day, and left him to get what he could from the passers-by.

So when he saw Peter and John coming, he held out his hand and begged for money.

Peter stopped, and so did John. Then Peter said, 'Look at us.' The man looked up hopefully. He had given up looking at people, only holding out his hand as each person passed in case they put something into it. So when he heard someone say, 'Look at us,' he suddenly felt he was being talked to as a person.

He held out his hand again only to hear Peter say, 'I have no money, but I will give you what I do have. In the name of Jesus Christ of Nazareth, get up and walk.'

Then he took the man's hand and pulled him up. Immediately his feet, which had never been any use, supported him, and he found himself standing on them for the first time in his life.

He could hardly believe it. He took a step to make sure. Then he jumped. That worked too, and before he knew where he was he was running and jumping beside Peter and John. They all went into the Temple together and stood in Solomon's Porch, where Jesus had stood talking to the people.

The man who had been cured shouted for joy as he went along, thanking God for his recovery, and everybody recognised him as the one who had sat for years at the gate unable to move.

'Why, what has happened?' they asked as they gathered round Peter and John. They were astonished and puzzled to see the once lame beggar standing straight and strong between his two new friends.

Peter had lived with Jesus through the experience of the Cross and now had the new power Jesus had promised. He no longer minded what people could do to him. This was a chance to tell the people the truth which they might not be so pleased to hear.

'Why are you all so surprised,' he asked, 'as if it was anything to do with us that this man can walk? God has shown you the power of His Son Jesus Christ, whom you insisted on having killed, even though Pilate would have let Him go.

'You chose to let a murderer go instead of Jesus, but though Jesus was killed God brought Him back to life. It was believing in the name of Jesus which made this lame man walk.'

Then Peter went on to say that he knew many people had not understood what they were doing by killing Jesus, but that they had no excuse for not understanding. The prophets had spoken for centuries about His coming, and they could have known what was going to happen.

As Peter was speaking the priests and the Captain of the Temple Police, with some of their friends, came up and joined the crowd. They heard talk of Jesus being still alive just when they thought they had got rid of Him. It would have to be stopped. They pushed their way through the crowd, arrested Peter and John, and took them to prison. It was evening by that time, so they decided to leave them there overnight and consider what to do. However, five thousand people had already heard Peter and John. They had believed them, and decided to join them.

The next morning the High Priest and the rulers of the people were gathered together, including many of the High Priest's own relations. They sent for the two apostles and asked them, 'Who told you that you might do all these things?'

Peter and John were not shaken. The Holy Spirit had given them courage, and they repeated that they had cured the man in the name of Jesus whom the priests and rulers had killed, and whom God had raised up again.

The lame man was there too, standing by Peter and John, so no one could say he had not been healed. The members of the Council were amazed that ordinary working men like Peter and John, who had had no special education, could now speak with such authority and courage to the people. The Council also recognised Peter and John as men who had been Jesus' own companions. They told them to leave the room while they talked the matter over.

'Whatever are we to do?' they said to each other when they were alone. 'It is quite clear that a wonderful thing has happened, and no one will believe us if we say that it is not true. Let us just tell them never again to speak to anyone in the name of Jesus.'

When Peter and John were told this they replied, 'You must judge for yourselves whether we should obey you or God. All we can do is to tell people what we have seen and heard with Jesus.'

The High Priest looked round. The crowd was behind these two men. The man who had been lame for forty years was there and walking about. Everyone was praising God for what He had done. If the priests had harmed Peter and John the people would have turned against them.

All they could do was to say once more, 'Do not mention Jesus again, or we shall punish you,' and then they let them go.

Those who gave everything—
and two who did not

AS soon as they had been set free the apostles went back to their friends. They told them what the chief priests and rulers had said, and then they thanked God for the power He had sent into the world with His Son Jesus.

They prayed together, and the Holy Spirit came to them again, so that each one was able to speak with courage.

They were also enabled to act with courage. They decided not to have any private possessions, but to put all their property together and share it out according to what each one needed.

A man called Joseph Barnabas from the island of Cyprus sold a farm and gave the money to the apostles for their work.

There were also two people whose names have lived on, not for what they gave, but for what they did not give. Their names were

Ananias and Sapphira. They too sold some land, and brought the money to Peter, but it was not the whole amount. They pretended to have given everything, but had really kept back what they wanted. It looked noble and self-sacrificing, but it was dishonest.

Peter had said he would be in a certain place to accept gifts, and in due course Ananias came and put down his money.

Peter did not thank him and say how good it was of him to bring it. He said, 'Ananias, why has Satan made you lie to the Holy Spirit, and keep back part of the price of the land? While you had it, it was still your own, and after it was sold it was in your power to do what you wanted with it. Why did you scheme in your heart like this? You have not lied to men, but to God.'

When Ananias realised that Peter had seen through all the pious pretence in him, it was such a shock that he fell down dead, and some young men carried his body away and buried it.

About three hours later Peter was still standing receiving gifts when Sapphira came in, not knowing what had happened. Peter gave her a chance to tell the truth, and said, 'Tell me if such and such a price was what you got for the land.'

Sapphira replied, 'Yes, that was the price.'

Then Peter said with great conviction, 'How is it that you and your

husband have agreed together to test the Spirit of God? The men who buried your husband are here, and they will bury you too.'

And it was as he said. The cutting shaft of truth was so strong that Sapphira could not stand it, and she too fell dead.

The people all around were much shaken. They saw that no one could trifle with God or lie to Him. Ananias and Sapphira had not died because they did not give all their money, but because they had pretended to give it in order that men might think well of them.

From then on only those who were ready to go all the way, in complete honesty of purpose and whole-hearted giving, joined the apostles. Even so these numbered thousands, and the numbers grew. Some people felt they grew at an alarming rate.

This body of determined men and women used to meet together in the part of the Temple called Solomon's Porch, and even those who were not brave enough to follow them admired their courage.

Many brought their sick friends out into the streets on beds and stretchers in the hope that Peter might touch them, or even that his shadow might fall on them and heal them. Crowds came out from the cities around Jerusalem too, bringing people sick in body and mind. All who came were healed.

They came in such numbers that the High Priest and his party, the Sadducees, felt that something must be done to show who was really in charge. The Sadducees were the party who rejected the idea that those who die rise again. They were furious when they saw how Christ had risen from the dead. So they had the apostles seized and thrown in prison.

The High Priest's party felt that this would put a stop to the activities of the men who seemed to them to be challenging their leadership and authority. But they reckoned without God. During the night an angel came and opened the doors, and let the prisoners out.

'Go back to the Temple,' said the angel, 'and tell the people about this new way of life.'

The apostles reached the Temple just as the sun was coming up, and started teaching, and talking to everyone just as if nothing had happened. In the meantime the High Priest had gathered together the leaders of the Council (or Sanhedrin) and the rulers of Israel. Officers were sent to fetch the prisoners, but when they reached the prison it was empty.

'We found the doors locked and guarded,' said these officers when they got back, 'but when we opened them there was no one inside.'

As they were speaking another man came to say, 'Do you know that the men you put in prison are in the Temple teaching the people?'

So this time a senior officer was sent with the soldiers to arrest these uncontrollable men a second time, but they did not dare treat them roughly for fear of being stoned by the crowd.

When they reached the Council Room the High Priest said, 'Did we not give you strict orders not to teach about this man? And yet you go on doing it all over Jerusalem, and making everyone think that His death was our fault.'

Peter and the others answered, 'We obey God and not man. You killed Jesus and God brought Him to life again. God has sent forgiveness through Him, and what is more we have ourselves seen all the things we are talking about.'

This made the rulers of the Council angrier than ever. They felt it was time to kill the apostles.

But one of the Pharisees called Gamaliel said, 'Men of Israel, be careful what you do to these men. Many people come forward for a while, and people follow them. Then they die and gradually the followers disappear. Why not let these men alone? If this is only the teaching of man it will come to nothing, but if it comes from God you cannot stop it. You will only find you are fighting against God.'

Gamaliel was one of those men who try to keep in with both sides, but what he said helped, and the other Pharisees and priests decided to take his advice.

So they had the apostles beaten, and then once more they told them never again to speak about Jesus, and sent them away.

The apostles went off full of joy that they had been allowed to suffer something of the pain and shame that Jesus had gone through in His lifetime. Then they went straight back to the Temple, and went on speaking exactly as before.

Stephen

I N Jerusalem, as in other cities, there were groups of Jews from different countries. They spoke different languages and each had its own synagogue or meeting place.

During the first years after Jesus had left, these groups all tried to live as one family. They shared their possessions, their meals and their whole life with each other.

After a while, however, feelings began to develop between them. Some of the Greek-speaking widows, for instance, complained that widows from the Hebrew-speaking community were getting more than their fair share of the food.

It soon became clear that some responsible men were needed to take on the feeding arrangements. So seven were chosen. They were men of wisdom who knew the power of the Holy Spirit, and were called deacons or servers.

One of these was called Stephen. He was a man of special faith and power, and great miracles happened wherever he went. He moved among the Greek-speaking Jews, not just handing out food, but speaking as clearly as the apostles did about the need for men to change.

Many of them did not like this. They were glad to have the food but found Stephen's directness and clear-sightedness uncomfortable. They argued furiously but were never able to get the better of him. His touch with God was so strong that whatever they said could not shake him. So they changed their tactics.

They spread many rumours about Stephen, until a terrific battle began to rage around him. He was arrested and brought before the Jewish Council of Elders or Sanhedrin.

False witnesses were bribed to swear that they had heard him say that this Person called Jesus was going to destroy the Temple and all the customs given by Moses.

But Stephen stood steadfastly before them, fearless, and with great serenity.

The High Priest, in charge of the proceedings, looked coldly at Stephen and asked, 'Are the things true that are said about you?'

Stephen did not answer directly. He pointed them to history.

He went back to the time of Abraham and reminded them of the whole story of God's Plan for the people of Israel. He reminded them of how Abraham had left his home in faith because God had told him to go, and how God gave him a new country and a son Isaac, long after he had given up expecting a child to be born to his old wife; how Joseph was sold as a slave into Egypt, and yet how God was with him and saved his family through him; how Moses had led his people out of Egypt into the wilderness, in faith that God would do what He had promised and give them a country. Then he showed them how, in spite of all that God had done for them, the people kept turning against Him and against the men He sent to help them. They had turned against Moses too. They had always wanted a God they could see.

'You always resist the Holy Spirit,' said Stephen. 'As it was with your fathers, so it is with you. They killed the men who said Jesus was coming, and when He came you betrayed and killed Him too. You had the Law but you have not kept it.'

Keeping the Law was a matter on which the Pharisees specially prided themselves, so they were beside themselves with rage at Stephen's words.

For years they themselves had taught about the Law and the Prophets. They knew the stories by heart, but had never thought of applying the truth in them to themselves.

They sat round and ground their teeth in fury, but Stephen, full of the Spirit's power, said 'Look, I can see the doors of Heaven open, and Jesus standing by His Father.'

At this, all the Council shouted him down and stopped their ears. They rushed at him in a body and dragged him out of the city to stone him to death. This they had absolutely no right to do. The Sanhedrin had no power to condemn anyone to death, still less to carry out the sentence. That was why they had had to get Pilate to pass the sentence of death on Jesus.

So what they did now was murder, but they did not stop to consider this.

They hustled Stephen to the place of execution. In order to throw their stones more easily they took off their coats and put them down by a young man called Saul, who came from Tarsus in Cilicia. As the stones were hurled at him from all sides Stephen said, 'Lord Jesus, take my spirit.'

Then he knelt down and said, loud enough for them all to hear, 'Please, God, do not blame them for this.'

Then, battered by the stones, he died.

And the young man called Saul willingly watched it all happen.

Philip and the Ethiopian Treasurer

AFTER Stephen's death a great persecution started. It was the end of living quietly together. Many had to escape to other cities, but they took their new faith with them. They included the men who had organised the meals, one of whom was called Philip.

With others, he went north to Samaria and made a tour of the villages there. People flocked to hear them, and Peter and John, who with the other apostles had stayed in Jerusalem, went up to help.

After a time they went back to Jerusalem, and Philip started with them.

Suddenly, however, God gave him the thought to go south along the road to Egypt. There seemed to be no particular reason for it, but Philip obeyed and went. As he went along the road, he saw an Ethiopian sitting in a chariot by the roadside, reading. Today he might have looked like an important official sitting in a Rolls Royce. He was in fact the Treasurer to the Queen of Ethiopia, a country which lies to the south of Egypt.

Philip did not know who he was, but the Holy Spirit said clearly to him, 'Go and get into that chariot.' So he did and found that the man in it was reading the words of the prophet Isaiah.

'Do you really understand what you are reading?' asked Philip.

The Ethiopian replied, 'How can I, unless someone explains it to me?' and he asked Philip to sit beside him and tell him about it.

Philip looked at the passage the stranger was reading and saw that it was Isaiah's description of the coming of someone who would be sacrificed for other people.

'Who is this person the prophet speaks of?' asked the Ethiopian Treasurer. 'Is it himself, or someone else?'

So Philip told him. By this time the chariot had driven on and they went on a long way together, while Philip told the whole story of Jesus, and what he himself knew about Him.

The Treasurer listened intently, and after a while they found themselves passing a well in the desert.

'Look,' said the Treasurer. 'Here is some water. What is to stop me being baptised?'

He was so clearly the man to whom Philip had been sent for a purpose, that they both got out of the chariot and Philip baptised him as he had been asked to do. Then, his work being done, they parted. The Ethiopian went home, and though we never hear of him again, he took the news of Jesus back to his country with him. Here it took root and grew from that time until today.

Saul (who became Paul)

OTHER people escaped after Stephen's death to the Syrian city of Damascus. So instead of the new faith and idea being stamped out they spread more quickly than before.

This worried the chief priests, and they looked round for a reliable man who would hunt these people down and destroy everything they believed in.

The man they chose was Saul of Tarsus, who had looked after the clothes of the murderers of Stephen. He seemed to be just the kind of person they needed. He was clever and passionate, hard and pitiless, and able to carry out their orders of going from house to house, dragging out both men and women and throwing them into prison.

Saul was a Jew. He came from the Cilician city of Tarsus in Asia Minor, where his father had become a Roman citizen. So he was a Roman as well as a Jew. His Roman name was Paul, but he was fiercely proud of being a Jew, and did not use the Roman form of his name. He had been brought up as a Pharisee, which was the strictest form of the Jewish faith, and he willingly carried out the orders of the chief priests to destroy everyone who put obedience to Jesus before obedience to them.

They hoped that this would discourage the men and women of what was by now called 'The Way', and make them think that it was both too difficult and too dangerous to follow.

Saul was like a dragon, breathing out threats and murder. One day he went to the High Priest in Jerusalem asking for letters which he could take to the rulers of the synagogues in the northern city of Damascus. These letters gave him permission to seek out the people of the Way in that city and bring them in chains to Jerusalem.

The High Priest readily gave him the letters, and Saul set off with the men he needed for the task. As he travelled along the road he was probably planning how to set about the terrible work he had undertaken. At the same time he had seen Stephen die, and it must have been a hard thing to get it out of his mind.

He and his companions had almost reached Damascus when

suddenly a light brighter than daylight shone around them.

Saul was dazzled. He fell on his knees and covered his eyes. As he crouched there he heard a voice say, 'Saul, Saul, why are you persecuting me?'

'Who are you, Lord?' he asked trembling, and the answer came back, 'I am Jesus and you are persecuting Me. It is hard for you to kick against the pricks.'

'The pricks' meant the pricks of the goad or sharp stick with which men urged on their animals. It hurt when the beasts resisted it as Saul had resisted Jesus.

Still trembling and astonished, Saul asked, 'What do you want me to do, Lord?'

Jesus answered, 'Get up and go to the city, and you will be told what to do.'

The men who were with Saul were terrified too. They had heard a voice, but could see no one. Saul was still lying on the ground, and they pulled him to his feet. When he stood up and opened his eyes he found that the brilliance of the light had blinded him, so they took him by the hand and led him into Damascus. There they left him at a house in a road called Straight Street.

The man who had breathed threats and death was blind and completely helpless. He did not know what to do, and prayed to be shown.

Saul sees with new eyes

THERE lived in Damascus, at this time, a follower of Jesus named Ananias. Three days after Jesus had spoken to Saul on the Damascus Road, He spoke also to Ananias by name and said, 'Go to the house of Judas in Straight Street and ask for Saul of Tarsus. He is there, praying, and he has had a vision of a man named Ananias coming and putting his hand on him to restore his sight.'

'But, Lord,' said Ananias, 'I have heard all about this man Saul. He has done terrible things to our people in Jerusalem, and has only come here to take us all to prison.'

Jesus answered, 'Go and do what I tell you, because I have specially chosen him to take news of Me to the Gentiles, and to kings, and to the people of Israel. I will show him all he has to suffer for My sake.'

The Jews called all the nations that were not Jews, Gentiles. They believed that God wanted them to keep apart from all non-Jewish people, so it was a totally new idea that a Jew, and a Pharisee at that, should be sent specially to the Gentiles.

Ananias, however, did as he was told. He went to the address in Straight Street, where he found Saul, who was still blind and had eaten nothing for three days. Laying his hands on him he said, 'Brother Saul, Jesus, who appeared to you on the way here, has sent me so that you may have your sight back and be filled with the Holy Spirit.'

Immediately something like scales fell from Saul's eyes, and he could see again. But he was weak from lack of food, so Ananias took him home and looked after him till he had recovered his strength.

Saul stayed in Damascus for a short time with the courageous band of men and women whom he had just been trying to stamp out. He went to the synagogue, not this time to arrest them, but to announce openly that he now knew that Jesus was the Son of God.

This caused a great stir.

'Surely this is the man who destroyed our friends in Jerusalem,' said people to one another. 'Has he not come here to arrest us too?'

Paul, in a letter written many years later, says that at this point he decided that he must be alone with God for a time.

'I consulted no human being,' he writes,* 'nor did I go to Jerusalem to see the men who were apostles before me, but I went to Arabia.'

Nobody knows exactly how long he stayed by himself in Arabia, but when he came back to Damascus after this time alone with God, he was sure of what God had called him to say and do.

He spoke boldly again in the synagogues and so ran up against the party of the chief priests whose orders he once used to carry out. They were dismayed to find him still in the ranks of the people they had employed him to put down, and decided that he had better be put down himself before his influence spread too far.

Saul, however, was alert. He heard of their plotting and of how the ambushes had been laid for him at all the gates of Damascus, to stop him from getting away. So his friends lowered him over the wall one night in a basket and he escaped to Jerusalem.

Here he searched out the men and women who had been trained by Jesus. But nobody would believe him or trust him. The disciples were terrified, and thought he had been sent among them as a spy.

Fortunately, one man, Joseph Barnabas, the Cypriot who had sold all his possessions, did believe

* Galatians (Chapter 1, verse 17).

him. Barnabas took him to the apostles and told them of Saul's brave stand in Damascus, after meeting Jesus on the way there.

Having listened to Barnabas, they were convinced that Saul wanted to fight with them and not against them, and he was accepted. He then spoke boldly in the synagogues about Jesus, not only to the Hebrew-speaking Jews but also to those who spoke Greek.

However, his troubles were far from over. For a while he went in and out freely among all the Jewish communities, telling them of what had happened to him. But the Greek Jews particularly resisted him. They made plans to kill him, and when Saul's friends heard of it, they realised that it was not safe for him to stay in Jerusalem. So they sent him back to his home town of Tarsus, where he stayed for some years.

No further persecutions broke out in Judæa for some time after this, and a surge of new life spread through the country.

Peter widens his horizon

MEANWHILE Peter was moving round the country from one Jewish village to another.

God's spirit was at work everywhere. In a seaport called Joppa, a woman named Dorcas had just died. She was generous and unselfish and had given her life to helping the needy. When her friends heard that Peter was in the neighbourhood, they asked him to come at once. They led him upstairs to the room where he found a group of widows and poor women whom Dorcas had cared for. They were holding in their hands the clothes she had made for them or their families while she was alive. With tears running down their cheeks, they held them out for Peter to see.

He said nothing but put all the weeping women out of the room. Then he knelt down and prayed. As he prayed Dorcas opened her eyes and sat up. Peter helped her to her feet and led her back to the mourning women outside the door, and there were great rejoicings all through Joppa.

Peter stayed on in Joppa for a time with a man named Simon. It was to be a turning point in Peter's life, and affected history too.

Peter was a Jew, and up to this time the battle between those who were for Jesus and those who were against Him had been waged entirely inside the Jewish nation. Some said He was the Messiah who had been sent to save the Jews. Others said He was not the Messiah at all. But nearly everyone thought that it was a purely Jewish question which had nothing to do with anyone else.

Someone was needed to break through this block in their minds, and the man God chose to do it was Cornelius, a Roman officer.

The Romans as a nation did not believe in one God. Like the Greeks they believed in many gods. If they wanted to win a battle they prayed to the god of war. If they wanted to be wise, they prayed to the goddess of wisdom, and so on. Above all, they believed in Rome and in themselves.

Cornelius may well have come to know about the real God from the Jews. He was stationed in their country and had grown to respect the

people, who had passed on their belief in God to him. He was generous too. He helped the poor and was known for his good works.

One day he was praying about three o'clock in the afternoon, when God spoke to him through an angel, who called him and said, 'Cornelius.' When Cornelius heard his name he looked up and saw the angel standing there.

'What is it, Lord?' he asked.

'God has heard your prayers,' said the angel, 'and He has seen all the good you have done. He wants you now to send two of your servants to Joppa. There they must ask for a man called Simon Peter who is staying with a tanner in a house by the sea-shore. He will tell you what to do.'

Then the angel left him, and Cornelius called two of his faithful servants, and an old soldier who had served him for many years. He told them what had happened and sent them to Joppa to find Peter.

Caesarea, where Cornelius lived, was on the coast north of Joppa, and it took the servants till noon the following day to get there. They arrived just as Peter was finishing his midday prayers on the flat roof of the house. It was nearly lunchtime and he was getting hungry, so, as his mind was rather on food, God spoke to him in a way that made him think. Suddenly it seemed to him that an enormous sheet was being let down from Heaven, full of all sorts of different animals. Everything you can think of was there. There were four-footed beasts, birds, and even creeping things like lizards, and as he looked at them he heard a voice saying, 'Come, Peter, kill one of these and eat.'

Peter had been taught to follow the rule of Moses about what to eat, and looking over the creatures in the sheet, he saw that there were many which Moses had forbidden his people to have as food.

'No, thank you, Lord,' he replied. 'I have never eaten anything common or unclean.'

At this the voice said, 'If I make anything clean, it is not for you to call it common.'

This happened three times, after which the sheet was taken back into Heaven, leaving Peter wondering what it could mean. While he was still wondering, the messengers from Cornelius knocked at the door of Simon the tanner's house, and asked if a man called Simon Peter was staying there.

Peter did not hear them, but the Holy Spirit let him know they had come, saying, 'Look, there are three men asking for you. Get up and go with them. Have no fear, for I have sent them.'

So Peter went to the door.

'I am the man you are looking for,' he said. 'Why have you come?'

They explained who Cornelius was, and how he had been told to send for Peter and hear what he had to say.

When Peter heard this he began to realise what the dream of the animals in the sheet had meant. As a Jew, he had never mixed with people who were not Jews. He never had anything to do with them. He believed that Jesus had been sent only to the Jewish nation, and that anyone outside it was, in a way, common and unclean as he had thought the animals were.

Through this dream, and the coming of the messengers, he began to understand that God's plan in sending Jesus was far wider than he had thought. Jesus came not for any one nation, but for the whole world. So though the servants who came with the message were not Jews, he asked them to come in and stay the night.

Peter goes to stay with Cornelius

THE next morning Peter left for Caesarea with the servants of Cornelius and took some of his own friends with him.

They arrived to find that Cornelius had invited quite a large party of his family and close friends to meet them. As soon as Cornelius saw Peter he fell on his knees before him, but Peter helped him to his feet saying, 'Stand up, I am only a man like you.'

'You know,' he said to the waiting guests, 'that by the laws of the Jewish people, we are not allowed to make friends with anyone who is not a Jew, but God has shown me that I should not think of other people as common or unclean. So as soon as I had your message I came at once. What was your purpose in asking for me?'

Cornelius then explained how the angel had given him Peter's exact name and address with instructions to send for him.

'So I sent word to you immediately,' said Cornelius, 'and now here we all are, and we want to hear whatever God tells you to say.'

'Truly,' said Peter, 'I see that God does not have favourites, but that in every nation He accepts the people who honour Him and live straight.'

Then he told them the story of Jesus, not in the way he had told it to the High Priest, but in a way suited to people who were hearing it for the first time. Cornelius and his friends had had nothing to do with killing Jesus, so Peter simply told them how Jesus had come and what He had done. He said the Jews had been responsible for His death, not even mentioning the part Pontius Pilate had played. Then he described how God had brought Jesus back to life.

'God raised Him up,' he said, 'and showed Him not to everyone but to those who were specially chosen. We ate and drank with Him

after He came to life again, and He told us to go and tell everyone that He had been sent to be the judge of the living and the dead, and that through Him all men can be forgiven.'

Cornelius and his friends believed Peter, and the Holy Spirit came into their hearts. The Jews who were present were surprised that the gift of the Holy Spirit should be given to people of another race, but Peter said, 'Why should not all these people be baptised who have received the Holy Spirit as we have?' He saw that the ideas he had had about his own nation being the only one to whom God could speak were out of date, so he let them go.

When word of this reached the rest of the apostles who had stayed in Jerusalem, they objected strongly. They sent for Peter when he got back and said, 'You went and ate with men who are not Jews,' and asked him to explain why he had done it.

So Peter told them the story of the animals in the sheet, how the messengers from Cornelius had arrived, how God had told him to go with them to Caesarea, and what had happened there.

'After all,' said Peter, 'if God gave these people the same gift as He gave us, who am I to stop Him from doing what He wants?'

This convinced the rest of the apostles. They stopped talking and were grateful that God had shown others as well as them how to find new life. They were honest and humble enough to change their minds, not over a matter where they knew they were wrong, but over something about which they were sure they were right.

Peter escapes from prison

MEANWHILE, what was called 'The Church in Jerusalem' was having a hard time. By 'The Church', I mean the people God had called, not just a building, and these people were once again being persecuted.

King Herod had ordered James, one of the twelve apostles, to be killed and this had been done. When he saw that it pleased certain of the Jews, he arrested Peter too and had him put in prison. He meant to keep him there till after Easter and then bring him out before the people as Pontius Pilate had done with Jesus. Sixteen soldiers were put on guard and Peter's friends could do nothing to help him but pray, which they did ceaselessly, together.

The days went by until the night Herod had intended to have him

brought out. Peter was asleep in his cell chained between two soldiers with guards on the door to make sure he did not escape.

Suddenly a bright light shone in the prison and Peter felt someone touch him and say, 'Get up quickly.' He looked up to see an angel standing beside him, and at the same time the chains fell off his hands.

The angel said, 'Dress, and put on your sandals.' Then he said, 'Wrap your cloak around you and follow me.'

Peter obeyed almost without knowing what he was doing. He thought he must be dreaming. However, he followed his guide and when they reached the iron gate that led into the city, it opened of its own accord and they went out into the street. Peter still did not know whether he was on his head or his heels, and the angel went with him down one street before leaving him.

By this time, Peter realised that he was not dreaming, but was actually out of prison standing in the road in the middle of the night, and he knew that he better make his way to safety.

He pulled himself together, and considered what he should do. He decided to go to the house of a woman called Mary, the sister of Barnabas, and the mother of a young man called John Mark.

Mary's house is thought to be the one in which Jesus ate the Last Supper with His friends. Her son John Mark may have been the young man with the linen sheet wrapped round him who was in the Garden of Gethsemane when Jesus was arrested. He escaped leaving the sheet in the hands of the men who came to take Jesus. The only mention of this is by Mark in his account of the story, which makes people think he wrote it about himself.

Anyway, his mother's house was the main meeting point for the friends of Jesus, and it was the obvious place for Peter to go to.

As they had undertaken to pray steadily for him right round the clock, many of them were there when he knocked on the door.

It was dangerous in that occupied country to open a door in the middle of the night without knowing who was outside. So a young girl called Rhoda went to see if she could tell who had come.

When she heard Peter's voice she was so excited that she never thought of letting him in, but rushed back to tell the others he was standing at the door.

'Nonsense!' they said. 'You must be mad.'

'No,' she replied, 'it's true.'

'It must be his ghost,' they said.

All this time a very real Peter was standing out in the street, and if any of King Herod's patrols had come by, they might well have arrested him again. So he went on knocking, until his friends finally decided to go and look.

To their amazement they found that their prayers had really been answered. Peter was standing there safe and sound.

They broke into cries of welcome and he had to sign to them to keep quiet and not rouse the whole neighbourhood.

He told them how he had been brought out of prison, and asked them to pass on the news. Then he went off to hide in another place.

When daylight came and the soldiers found that Peter had gone, there was, as the Bible says, 'no small stir' among them as to what could have become of him.

The King ordered a search to be made, and when Peter could not be found Herod had all the guards killed. Then he left the city. He wanted to go somewhere where he could show that he was master. So he went to Caesarea which depended on him for food supplies. Here he called a great assembly and spoke to the people. They were so afraid of him that they fell down before him saying, 'It is the voice of a god—not of a man.'

But as the cry went up, Herod was struck with a sudden and terrible illness.

The man who had tried to master God fell dead.

God's plan of campaign

MORE than fourteen years had passed since the rushing wind of the Spirit had swept through a house in Jerusalem, and a hundred and twenty unknown people had been changed into fire-brands who would stop at nothing. That wind was going to blow them to places far afield.

As Jesus had said to Nicodemus, the timid ruler who came to Him at night, 'The Spirit of God is like a wind which goes where it wants. Nobody knows where it comes from or where it will go next.'

Though we may not always understand it, the Holy Spirit is the most intelligent force in the world. The plans made by Him have a way of working out when people obey Him. For instance, what had happened to Peter and to Saul was part of His plan to reach out from Judæa and Samaria to the furthest parts of the earth and make the rule of God the most powerful force in the world.

Neither Peter nor Paul knew this at first. They did not even know each other. Both had their own ideas of what God wanted and He had to break into their lives in His own way to make them change their minds. If He had not done so, it is hard to see what would have brought them together.

Peter was a worker—a fisherman. He was impulsive and sometimes unreliable. Saul had been to a university. He had a brilliant mind, but a closed heart, and did not mind seeing the suffering and even death of people who thought differently from him. Something had to happen to both of them if they were ever going to find a united purpose, and it did happen as we have seen.

God used Cornelius the Roman to break through Peter's narrow national idea of God's Plan. Jesus Himself spoke to Saul and changed his whole outlook on life.

So you must picture this atomic action of the Holy Spirit going off like an explosion in unexpected places; unexpected anyway to the men who were trying to track it down and put it out of action. No one knew where it would break out next.

Many people who had met the apostles in Jerusalem went to distant places. So did others who had fled when the Jewish authorities had Stephen stoned. Everywhere they went they told the story of Jesus, but as most of them had left before they heard of Peter's dream about the animals in the sheet, they tended to tell it only to the Jews.

Some went to the island of Cyprus, others to the great seaport of Antioch which was also an important trading city. Roads reached out from there all over the world. Naturally those who had learned about Christ from His Jewish friends in Judæa spoke about Him mainly to all their Jewish friends in Antioch. Gradually the news spread to the Greeks and Greek-speaking people there, and a large number began to turn to what was still called just 'The Way'.

In Antioch for the first time they began to be known as Christians. It was a name which had nothing to do with being a Greek or a Jew or a Roman. It started as a nickname, but came to stand for people who put Christ Himself before their own plans and points of view, and this gave them strength and unity.

The news of the tremendous popular response reached Jerusalem, and the leaders there sent Barnabas to Antioch to investigate. He found more people to teach and train than there were teachers, and he thought of his friend Saul who was still at home in Tarsus.

Saul was needed, so Barnabas went and brought him back to help at Antioch.

If you look at the map you will find Tarsus not far from Antioch, just round the corner of the north-eastern end of the Mediterranean.

Saul was ready. He was convinced and convincing, though he was always to remember his earlier record of cruelty. It kept him humble, and wondering, that he should have been chosen to work with men whom Jesus had known and trusted.

It gave him a certainty that no one is too far gone to change and be forgiven for the past.

He and Barnabas stayed in Antioch for a year teaching the crowds who flocked to them.

While Barnabas was there, some teachers came from Jerusalem. One of them, named Agabus, brought a warning from God that a famine was soon going to break out across the known world of that time. The group in Antioch, who were perhaps better off now than their friends in Jerusalem, decided to raise a fund which would give them something to fall back on when the bad times came. It was rather like the way that Joseph, in his day, was prepared by God for the famine in Egypt and was able to save both the Egyptians and his own people.

When all the gifts had come in, the Antiochans asked Barnabas and Saul to take them with their greetings to Jerusalem.

Barnabas and Saul go to Cyprus

WHEN Barnabas and Saul had handed over the money for the Famine Fund to their friends in Jerusalem, they went back to Antioch, taking with them Barnabas' nephew John Mark. There they worked with several other men. Among them were two dark-skinned North Africans; Symeon, called 'The Black', and Lucius from Cyrene. A third was the foster-brother of the reigning King Herod—a son of the Herod who had just died.

Together they asked the Holy Spirit what the next moves were to be. They prayed and cut down their food, so as to be able to think more clearly, and the Holy Spirit gave them clear direction, 'Call out Barnabas and Saul for the work I have given them to do.'

He also showed them that the next stage of His Plan was to be the island of Cyprus and they asked John Mark to go with them.

If it is true that he was the young man who followed Jesus and His friends to the Garden of Gethsemane in the middle of the night, he must have had initiative and courage. So when Barnabas and Saul asked him to join the expedition to Cyprus, he accepted, and they all set sail together. Barnabas was a Cypriot and took the lead, as it was his home country.

They landed at the eastern end of the island and went along the length of it, speaking in the Jewish synagogues, till they reached Paphos at the western end, where the Roman governor lived. His name was Sergius Paulus and he had a Jewish adviser called Elymas. The local people called Elymas 'The Wizard'. He had some sort of hold over Sergius Paulus and tried to influence him, as many men still try to influence the leaders of nations nowadays.

Sergius Paulus, however, had a mind of his own. He sent for

37

Barnabas and Saul and asked what message God had for him, but Elymas tried to stop them. He knew that if the governor began to obey the Holy Spirit, his own power over him would be gone.

At this moment Saul stepped forward into new authority. He was not prepared to put up with a man who wanted to destroy someone else's faith.

We read that 'Saul, who is also called Paul, was filled with the Holy Spirit'. Looking Elymas straight in the eye he said to him, 'You are one of Satan's children—when will you stop trying to twist the right ways of God? You shall be blind for a while to teach you a lesson.' Immediately a mist fell over the eyes of Elymas, and he looked for someone to lead him by the hand.

Paul had also become blind when he first heard the truth about himself. This was perhaps the only way for God to teach Elymas too. It must have been hard for a man who was used to having so much power over others, not even to be able to walk about without help from someone else.

For Paul this marked another milestone. In his long time of thought and quiet earlier, he had learned from God that he was to proclaim what he calls 'God's open secret' to every part of the world of his day.

He was to help people everywhere to understand 'the breadth and length and depth and height' of God's love for all men everywhere. Rome with her soldiers and her law ruled the world Paul knew, and the Holy Spirit would need to win control of the men who controlled the different peoples of that world.

In Cyprus Paul stood face to face for the first time with the Roman governor of the island, who was also called Paul, and it was not Saul the Jew who spoke to him, but Paul the Roman citizen. Sergius Paulus was a Roman soldier and diplomat who moved from place to place, and could bring new life to thousands of people if he himself came under the Holy Spirit's direction.

The next stage of the journey shows Paul, both Jew and Roman citizen, moving through the Roman empire with its network of roads and cities running all round the Mediterranean, and centring on Rome.

Paul, like Peter, had his eyes opened to wider horizons. He saw that he must move to the mainland and work along the great trade routes which led to Rome.

Barnabas agreed to go with him, but John Mark refused. We are not told why. He went as far as the mainland with them, to the harbour of Perga, and then left to go back to Jerusalem.

Paul's eyes were on Rome. How did this empire of Rome come into being?

From Settlement to Empire

ABOUT eight hundred years before Christ, some scattered groups of people were living on seven hills sticking out of the marshes by the Tiber. They joined themselves into one community, which they called Rome. In after years, the Romans said that their first king, whom they called Romulus, built a city wall round the central hill in 753 B.C.

From this small settlement the Romans reached out to the lands all round the Mediterranean Sea, up into western Europe, and into the island of Britain. They swallowed up what was left of the Empire of Alexander the Great, and inherited Greek as a common language for all the countries over which he had ruled.

Alexander himself had died just under three hundred years before the birth of Christ, and Rome had been founded about four hundred years before that.

So in seven hundred years the power of Rome had grown and spread over North Africa, France (or Gaul as it was then called), parts of Germany, Britain, Greece, and the countries round the eastern end of the Mediterranean where Jesus was born and where he lived during His life-time.

Just before He was born the ruler of these vast territories took the title of Emperor, and he is the Caesar Augustus who ordered the census to be taken which led Mary and Joseph to Bethlehem.

Rome was the centre of power; but Greece had long been the centre of learning, and continued to be so through the Roman occupation. In fact Roman nobles often sent their sons to be educated at Greek universities.

So Greece was a key point for winning the empire to new ideas.

The Roman empire was interwoven with various strands. There was the great pattern of the empire itself, with its roads and cities, there were the language and the universities of the Greeks, and there were the Jewish communities or settlements.

These communities had started as a result of Jews escaping from various invasions of their own country, and there were recognised groups of them with synagogues in every Roman city. Paul always went to them first, and though they did not always accept him, he was able to establish a foothold through them.

He himself had a natural link with all sides of the life of the Empire. He was a Roman citizen. He was brought up in the Greek city of Tarsus, and he was a Jew who had studied under the best Jewish teachers in Jerusalem.

Paul and Barnabas in Galatia

AFTER John Mark had left them, Paul and Barnabas moved to the mainland. It was made up of several large provinces. One of the largest was called Asia, and when Paul speaks of being in Asia this is the place he means, not India or China. Another province was inhabited by a tribe of Gauls, and was known because of them as Galatia. The central town in this whole area was Antioch in the province of Pisidia.

This was not the Antioch Paul and Barnabas had started from to go to Cyprus, which was Antioch in Syria. (You can see where all these places were by looking at the map on page 48.)

There were four towns within reach of each other; Antioch in Pisidia, Iconium, Lystra and Derbe. Paul and Barnabas now moved to and fro between these towns which were at the crossroads of the trade routes running east and west, and north and south. So it was an important area. Any idea which captured the minds of its people could be taken far and wide by the many merchants and travellers who daily went about their business there.

Paul and Barnabas had a number of adventures in these cities, and were received in many different ways. They were met sometimes with understanding, sometimes with arguments, and sometimes with stones. Some people moved, so to speak, into a higher gear in their lives. Others wanted to stay in low gear. Those who were against changing gear hit back. Paul expected this, and it never put him off. He knew he was in a war, and that no one can fight wars on the cheap.

He went back and back to all these places, no matter what sort of reception he had had in them before. He went on moving as the Holy Spirit told him, and ran into all sorts of people as he went.

In Pisidian Antioch he and Barnabas went, as usual, first to the Jews. Some of the Gentile people who were listening at the back of the synagogue begged Paul to come back and speak to them the following week. This he did, and practically the whole city turned out. When the Jews saw how many Gentiles had come they became fiercely jealous of Paul and Barnabas attracting such a crowd. They contradicted Paul and tried to break up the assemblies where he spoke. They told lies about him and Barnabas, and stirred up even the most respectable people, including the leaders of the city, to have them thrown out.

So Paul and Barnabas said, 'Very well. We came to you first, because you are our own people, but if you will not listen, we shall go to the Gentiles.'

The same thing happened in Iconium, but at Lystra when they had healed a lame man the crowd thought that they were Greek gods who had miraculously come to earth. Paul and Barnabas had some difficulty in stopping them from arranging a sacrifice in their honour. They never passed unnoticed.

Men who did not want to change their ways were prepared to kill those who went the way of the Spirit, as they had killed Jesus and

Stephen and many others. These men were by no means only to be found among the Jews. In Iconium the Jews who did not want to change enlisted the Gentiles, and pursued Paul and Barnabas from one town to another. Even in Lystra, where they had such a warm, if mistaken, welcome, the tide soon turned and Paul was  stoned. He was dragged out of the city and left for dead. Fortunately his friends found that he was alive. By the next day he had recovered enough to move to Derbe with Barnabas.

Nothing daunted, the two of them went back over the same ground again, Antioch, Iconium, Lystra and Derbe, encouraging and training their new recruits. Then they moved south to the coast.

They told everyone that they were not offering them an easy life; but everywhere brave men and women joined them. Then passing through Perga once more, they took a ship from the port of Attalia back to Syrian Antioch.

So the outposts of the Way grew in numbers, and Paul and Barnabas took with them to Antioch their report of all that God had done, particularly in reaching the Gentiles, and showed how the road to Rome was opening up.

The foolish Galatians

SOME time later, Paul was in the Greek town of Corinth. News reached him that teachers from Jerusalem had followed after him trying to prove that the Law of Moses must be kept in every detail before anyone could find Jesus.

The Galatians were a people who moved quickly from one mood to another. At one moment the crowd had taken Paul for a god, and almost immediately afterwards had set on him with stones. His

Galatian friends did not find it easy to stick to what he had taught them.

When he heard that they were being swayed by these other teachers who said that he had no real authority, and no official position, he sat down and wrote them a letter.

'I am astonished that you are so unstable,' he wrote, 'that you turn away from the God who called you and swing to different teachings. What I told you about Jesus was not passed on to me by any human being. I had it from Jesus Himself. You know what I was like before, and how I persecuted people even of my own race, because I was so sure they all had to keep the Law. But God in His goodness showed me His Son, so that I could take the news of Him to the Gentiles.'

Then he went on to tell them about the years he had spent alone in Arabia, and how it was only after this time that he even met and spoke to Peter. All he learnt in Arabia was straight from God and could not have been learnt from men.

Paul knew with absolute certainty that God Himself had called him, for the special purpose of telling the Gentile nations about Jesus Christ. Great truths had been entrusted to him about God and His Son which could not be altered to suit other people's points of view.

'Fourteen years after I first met Peter,' he said, 'I went up to Jerusalem again. Barnabas came with me and a Greek called Titus. I told Peter and the others in Jerusalem exactly what I was telling the Gentiles and they agreed with me. Though Titus was a Gentile, no one insisted on his keeping all the Law, though there were some people who tried to pin him down to it.'

Paul was trying to show his friends in Galatia that he had learnt the lesson they needed to learn, which was to obey God rather than to please men. He told them of how Peter had once slipped back into getting on comfortably with people instead of running the risk of being unpopular.

'Peter came down to see me at Antioch,' Paul writes. 'We all ate together, Jews and Gentiles, including Peter himself. Then some men from Jerusalem arrived and Peter at once stopped eating with the Gentiles in order to try and please these men. I challenged him at once in front of everybody. I made it absolutely plain that a man is saved by believing and trusting in Jesus Christ, not just by doing what the Law says. If men can become good simply by trying to obey the Law in every detail, then Jesus gave His life in vain.'

Then Paul goes on to say, 'It is not just the Law that keeps me straight now, it is Jesus. O foolish Galatians! who has bewitched you, you who have heard all about Jesus?'

He explains to them that though the Law shows people where they have gone wrong, it does not give them the power to go straight.

'You knew God when I was with you before,' he says. 'Why do you want to turn back to old ways which I thought you had left behind? You almost make me feel that I wasted my time on you. I want you to be free; not free to do exactly as you please, but free to serve each other. As a matter of fact, the whole Law can be put into one sentence, "Love your neighbour as yourself." But if you snap and snarl and quarrel, you will only destroy one another.

'You are not free to do as you please, anyway. Either you obey the tempers and longings of your body, or you obey the Holy Spirit. If you lead the life of the Spirit then you will not be run by your body, which gets you into all sorts of trouble: impurity, jealousy, drunkenness, people taking sides against each other, and such like.

'You simply cannot find God if you live this way.

'On the other hand, when the Holy Spirit takes root in people, new qualities begin to grow in them—love, joy, peace, good temper, kindliness, generosity, faithfulness, gentleness, self-control. There is no law against any of these.

'If you bear one another's burdens you will obey the law of Christ. So make no mistake. You cannot fool God. You will reap what you sow. Things for the body which will die, or things for the spirit which will live forever.'

As if to sum up all he has been saying, he writes at the end, 'The Grace of our Lord Jesus Christ be with you all—and with your spirit.'

44

Are men to live by rules?

IN Syrian Antioch they ran into more trouble. The news of the great advance among the Gentiles had reached Jerusalem, and what might be called 'the question of the animals in the sheet' came up again.

Certain people came from Judæa, which was a Jewish country, to insist that all Gentile recruits enlisted by Paul and Barnabas should be made to keep the laws laid down by Moses.

Paul and Barnabas did not agree. They had seen with their own eyes God's Power changing the lives of people who had never even heard of the Law of Moses. They knew that these people were needed as much as the Jews in God's growing Plan for the whole world. There was much discussion and argument, but it led nowhere. So it was decided that Paul and Barnabas should go to a Council in Jerusalem and talk the matter over with Peter and the others there.

As Paul and Barnabas went through the villages, on the way to Jerusalem, they gave the news of what was happening among the Gentiles, and the villagers rejoiced at the news. No one raised any objections until they reached Jerusalem itself. Then a number of delegates to the Council who, like Paul, had been brought up as Pharisees, stood up and protested.

They were followers of Jesus and the Holy Spirit, but had started with the Law of Moses. This, they said, could not be by-passed. So Peter, who had been through it all in his own life, rose to his feet and said, 'You know God chose me to be the first through whom the Gentiles would hear and believe His message. He who reads the hearts of all confirmed this by giving them the Holy Spirit as He gave it to us. In giving them clean hearts through faith He made no difference between them and us. Why give them burdens to bear which many of us have found too heavy?'

'Surely,' he said, 'Jesus can come into their hearts as much as He comes into ours.'

No one had anything to say to this and there was complete silence.

So Paul and Barnabas took the opportunity of retelling the story of all that God had done among the Gentiles during the past weeks.

When they had finished, James, an older apostle, spoke out.

'God certainly called our people,' he said, 'and I am sure we should not make extra difficulties for others who are beginning to find Him. I suggest we should write a letter telling them to avoid unclean food and impurity. They can hear the Law of Moses any day in the synagogue, if they want to know what it says.'

This was agreed to by everyone and a letter was written to Antioch explaining these points. It was given to Paul and Barnabas to take back. Two other men called Judas and Silas went with them to represent the gathering in Jerusalem, and show that they had all really reached a united decision.

This letter encouraged the people in Antioch. They had never, anyway, spent their time over the points of disagreement between Jews and non-Jews, so that a strong and growing force had been built there.

After a time, Judas went back to Jerusalem, but Paul and Barnabas stayed in Antioch with Silas.

Paul loses two, but finds three

PAUL stayed in Jerusalem for a time after the Council meeting but soon he started on his next journey, which was in the end to lead him to so many unexpected places.

After a short stay in Antioch, Paul said to Barnabas, 'Shall we go back to our friends in the cities where we were before, and see how they are getting on?'

Barnabas agreed and said he would like his nephew John Mark to come too. But John Mark had left them in Cyprus, and Paul thought it would be unwise to take someone who might again decide to go home just when he was most needed.

This led to a sharp disagreement.

Barnabas refused to go without his nephew. Paul refused to go with him. So Barnabas went back to Cyprus, taking John Mark.

It must have been a blow to Paul to lose the man who had first stood up for him. Barnabas had recommended him to the apostles, and had brought him from Tarsus to build a united force at Antioch. Some time later, however, John Mark came back. Peter seems to have taken him on and helped him to find a stronger faith. Peter also helped him to write the story of Jesus which is called St Mark's Gospel, much of it probably in Peter's own words. Later still, Mark went back to Paul too. But this was still in the future.

So Paul took Silas as his companion and they set off together through Paul's home country of Cilicia, and on to the now familiar cities of Lystra and Derbe.

His work was winning and enlisting people. Just as Jesus had taken a group around with Him, training them as He went and then sending them out on their own responsibility, so Paul was always on the look-out for people to carry on the fight.

What he was doing in fact was raising an army, and if you explore the Book of the Acts you will see a pattern being woven not only of places but of people. I remember trying so hard when I was at school to trace where Paul was going that I never took in what he was doing.

It is clear that in every town he went to, he enlisted men and took them on with him to the next place. Sometimes he sent one of them ahead to prepare for his coming. Sometimes he left someone behind to carry on the training he had begun.

When he reached Lystra at the beginning of this new expedition,

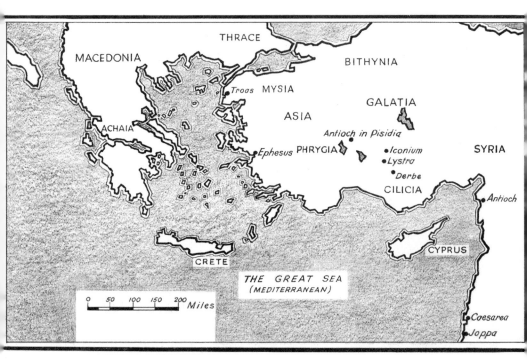

he was joined by a young man called Timothy whose mother was Jewish and his father Greek. As his father was probably dead, Timothy lived with his mother and grandmother, and Paul knew the whole family. He had been to Lystra twice before and may well have met them on one of these earlier visits.

Timothy knew about Paul, too, after all the riots and commotion that had gone on around him. He must have seen what to expect if he decided to join him but he was a young man of spirit and when Paul asked him to come, he accepted.

So, with Silas, the party was now three.

They started on what Paul thought was going to be another journey through Galatia and Phrygia, still going first to the Jewish communities in each place. For a long time Paul felt bound to give his own people the first chance of taking God's plan the next step forward. At the same time he took with him the letter written at the Council in Jerusalem, which made it clear that what he was talking about was a way of life for everyone, everywhere. It was not a movement or society which was for some and not for others.

He started west through the province of Phrygia, and as he had never gone as far as the northern provinces of Mysia and Bithynia, decided to go there next.

You can see from the map that anyone having moved west from Lystra and the towns round about, would reach Phrygia, and then, heading north, would be bound to reach Mysia and Bithynia, passing through the central province of Asia.

It seemed the obvious thing to do, but Paul had reckoned without the plan that had been worked out by the Holy Spirit. Try as he might he found himself absolutely prevented from getting on to Bithynia, or even teaching on the way there. Generally he spoke and taught wherever he went, but in Asia this guiding Spirit would not let him stop, but led him on as far as Mysia. There with Silas and Timothy he tried to go on into Bithynia, but the Holy Spirit stopped him.

So Paul and his party turned west again and seemed to be driven on without stopping through Mysia, till they reached the port of Troas. After that there was nowhere further to go. The land came to an end, and there was nothing ahead of them but the sea.

Puzzled by this complete upsetting of all his plans, Paul fell asleep one night in Troas wondering what to do next, and as he slept he

dreamt that he saw a man who called to him saying, 'Come over to Macedonia and help us.'

This was what he had been waiting for, without knowing it. Macedonia, or northern Greece, was the country which lay across the sea from Troas. The man he had seen in his dream was a Macedonian, and Paul had come to know a man of Macedonia during the days of waiting in Troas. This man's name was Luke and he was a doctor. He became Paul's faithful friend and companion from that time on.

He wrote the account of the first impact of the Holy Spirit, from which these stories are taken. It is called the Acts of the Apostles, but it is mostly about Paul who was the first man to go into action and show that Jesus came for the whole world, not just for people who called themselves Christians. There were no 'Christians' anyway when He died. He lived and died for people who had never heard of Him.

Luke did not go everywhere with Paul himself, but he shows when they were together by writing of the party as 'we'. And this is how we get the first hint of his existence.

He writes, 'As soon as *he* had seen the vision, *we* tried immediately to reach Macedonia, convinced that God had called *us* to take them the Good News.'

So Paul, Silas, Timothy and Luke sailed for Macedonia. They took a ship across the stretch of water separating Asia Minor from what today is part of Europe, and landed at Philippi in northern Greece.

Paul and Silas arrested at Philippi

THEY landed at the port of Philippi, knowing no one, but on the shore they met a group of women collecting shellfish, which were the raw materials for the local industry of making purple dye. Paul started talking to them, and a woman called Lydia, who sold the finished dye, was so interested that she asked Paul and all his friends to stay with her.

But they soon ran into trouble again. There was a slave girl who had a curious power of knowing what was going on in people's

minds. It was a kind of thought-reading, but it was not a power given by God. It simply made her able to do tricks with her mind, which her masters found very useful.

They took her about reading people's thoughts and charged a good price, so that they were on the way to becoming extremely rich.

Paul and Silas were going to the synagogue one morning with Luke and Timothy, when they met this girl. She immediately turned and followed them, saying, 'These men are servants of the most high God, who show us the way we can be saved.'

Paul paid no attention to her at first, but she followed them about for several days saying it over and over again, till he saw that it was a kind of madness.

It was not the Holy Spirit talking to her, but an evil spirit, and it saddened him that anyone should be making money out of this half-crazy girl. So he stopped and said to the evil spirit in her mind, 'I command you in the name of Jesus Christ to come out of her', and immediately the power of thought-reading left her.

She became an ordinary girl, instead of a freak, and her masters were furious. They saw that they were now going to lose money, so they seized Paul and Silas and brought them before the magistrates.

Though the crowd were all conquered people under the rule of Rome, when they saw that they were in danger of going out of business they all became very keen on being Romans.

'These men are Jews,' they complained. 'They are making a disturbance and starting customs which are against the Roman law.'

The magistrates, who do not seem to have tried particularly hard to find out whether this was true, ordered Paul and Silas to be beaten and put in prison.

The jailer was told to put them in the inner prison with their feet in the stocks and guard them carefully. The news of how Peter had got away from the prison in Jerusalem may have reached them. Anyway they were taking no chances.

Paul and Silas did not worry. They prayed and they sang so that all the other prisoners could hear them. Then suddenly at midnight there was a terrific earthquake. The doors burst open and the chains fell off all the prisoners.

The jailer, terrified, tried to kill himself. He knew what happened to guards who let people escape. But Paul called to him, saying, 'Do not harm yourself. We are all here.'

The jailer was astonished. He called for a light, and saw that it was true.

'Oh Sirs,' he said, 'what can I do to be saved?'

They told him that Jesus could save him and his whole household.

So though it was still the middle of the night the jailer took them to his house, where he gathered his family together to hear about the new explosive power which had come into the world. He washed his prisoners' wounds and they in turn baptised him and all his household.

Then he gave them a good meal, and it was a time of rejoicing all round.

You might have thought that once the meal was over Paul and Silas would have got away while the going was good, but in fact they decided to stay.

The next morning the magistrates sent word to them that they might leave, and evidently thought they would accept gratefully.

But when the jailer gave

them the message they replied, 'Not at all. We have been beaten in public without a trial, though we are Roman citizens. Do they think they can send us away without anyone knowing? Let them come and fetch us themselves.'

When the magistrates heard that their prisoners were Roman citizens they were badly shaken. They hurried to the prison and asked them politely if they would be good enough to leave the city quietly, which Paul and Silas did, after calling on Lydia to say goodbye.

They themselves went on along the main route which led to Rome, but they seem to have left Luke in Philippi to help the Philippians, because at this point the story says 'they' instead of 'we'.

So now they had established a base, or outpost, in what is today Europe, and went on through Greece.

Riots drive Paul south to Athens

PAUL, Silas and Timothy went from Philippi to Thessalonica, the next large town along the coast, and here the Greeks came in crowds to hear them. The Jewish colony again became furiously jealous. They had not accepted the idea of Jews mixing with the Gentiles, and started a riot, so Paul's friends decided to send him away secretly by night, with Silas and Timothy, to Berea, a town further south where they were warmly welcomed.

The Berean Jews were much more ready to learn, and made no objections to the Greeks joining them.

When the news got back to Thessalonica that the Jews and the Greeks had together welcomed Paul, his attackers pursued him and started another riot. So the Bereans took Paul on to Athens. Silas and Timothy stayed behind to keep an eye on the situation, until Paul sent a message asking them to join him as soon as possible.

As he had some days alone in Athens before they came, Paul wandered round the city looking at the sights and watching the people. The more he saw, the less satisfied he was with it. Athens was the home of learning. It was the most highly cultured and educated city in the world of Paul's day. People came to its teachers from all over that world. Yet everywhere he went he saw idols and altars.

The Athenians had no idea of there being only one God. Nor did they think of their own gods as beings who cared for them and wanted to help them. Gods, they thought, were powerful and wonderful, but also rather crotchety and bad-tempered, and it was

important not to make them angry. In spite of being so well-educated, the Athenians lived in constant fear of these gods and goddesses. Each had his or her own altar and statue, and in case there was one they had missed, and whose feelings might be hurt, they put up an extra altar and wrote on it: TO THE UNKNOWN GOD.

Paul came across this extra altar one day and thought it would give him a chance to speak to the people, and tell them what he knew from his own experience of the real God. Undiscouraged by what he had been through before, he spoke in the synagogue, and held open-air discussions in the market-place. But everyone seemed to be empty of thought, and interested in nothing but endless arguments. Having no faith, they were always chasing some new idea to see if it made any more sense than the last.

After a while Paul attracted the attention of some more thoughtful men. They took him to a famous assembly place called Mars Hill, where they asked him to speak about his new ideas.

He thought he had better begin with something they had all seen and knew about, so he said, 'You men of Athens certainly are a most religious lot. I see you even have an altar to an unknown God. I have come here to tell you who this unknown God is. This God actually made the whole world, and everything in it. He cannot possibly live in temples made by human beings, and you cannot give Him anything He needs, because He is the one who gives you everything you need; life and breath and everything else. We belong to His family, not to statues of gold or silver or stone that we have made ourselves. Of course you made them because you did not know, and God does not mind that kind of mistake, but now He wants to change your ways. He is going to judge the world by a Man whom He has sent. And He has proved that this is true by raising that man from the dead.'

As soon as the Athenians heard of someone being raised from the dead, there were jeers and laughter from some of the crowd, but others were thoughtful, and said, 'We should like you to tell us more about this.'

Certain people joined Paul, but on the whole the Athenians preferred to stay in the world of ideas and arguments. So when Silas and Timothy arrived soon afterwards from Berea, they considered what to do next. They decided that Silas and Timothy should go back to Thessalonica, but that Paul should again move on ahead, this time to the neighbouring city of Corinth.

Corinth and the Corinthians

IN Corinth Paul met a tent-maker called Aquila, and his wife
Priscilla. They were Jewish refugees from Rome. The Emperor
Claudius had ordered all Jews to leave his capital, and these two had
come and settled in Corinth.

As Paul was also a tent-maker, for everyone was brought up to a
trade of some kind, he stayed with Priscilla and Aquila, and worked
with them. Silas and Timothy joined him, having gone back to
Thessalonica to see how things were going there since the riots.

They found him speaking in the synagogue every week both to the
Jews and the Greeks, and working with the tent-makers in between.
Silas and Timothy's report made Paul decide to write a letter to the
Thessalonians to help them through the difficulties they were facing.
The two younger men worked on it with him. It was part of their
training. First they had been left to deal with a situation on the spot,
and then he showed them how to go on keeping in touch by letter.

They wrote two letters, as far as we know, and from the first we learn what Timothy had been doing.

'We thought the best plan,' Paul says in the letter, 'was for me to stay at Athens alone while Timothy . . . was sent to encourage you and strengthen your faith. We did not want any of you to lose heart at the troubles you were going through, but to realise that we Christians must expect such things. Actually we did warn you what to expect when we were with you, and our words have come true as you know. . . . But now Timothy has come straight from you to us with a glowing account of your faith and love. . . . How these things have cheered us in all the miseries we were going through.'

This is a new Paul speaking. He had come a long way from the cold unfeeling keeper of the Law who had watched Stephen's terrible death, and had been ready to see the same thing done to others. He had become a man of deep understanding, and his letters show the change that had taken place in him.

Paul, in a passage which is as living today as it was then, also helped his Thessalonian friends to understand what death really is. How to those who love Jesus, it is only a falling asleep from which they will wake to be with God. He gave them simple instructions about how to live. To mind their own business, to work with their hands, not to defraud anyone, to keep clear of impurity. This may sound obvious, but many of these teachings were completely new, particularly among Paul's Greek friends.

He knew what people missed when they turned their backs on what Jesus was trying to give them. He himself had been given a new nature, which was something he could never have done for himself. He had become a new man. He had a new heart and a new mind. He longed for everyone to know of the riches God had given him, and was ready and waiting to give all mankind.

Unfortunately, many of the men who, like him, had been trained in the Law, did not like the new Paul. They preferred him as he was before. He upset all their ideas of what was important and what was not. He kept steadily before them the fact that they had killed Jesus, the long-awaited Messiah, and this his fellow-Pharisees could not and would not bring themselves to face. So they did to Paul much of what he had earlier done to others.

It made his first visit to Corinth a stormy one. Though things had started quietly enough, after a while the Jews again refused to listen to him. He told them as usual about Jesus being the Messiah, and one day as he was speaking in the synagogue, they turned against him.

'Very well,' he said. 'I shall go to the Gentiles.'

So saying he went out of the synagogue to the house of a Roman who lived next door. This sobered the leader of the synagogue, who followed him with his whole family, and in so doing rallied a number of Corinthians, who began to take a stand with Paul.

Soon there was another attack. A group of Jews seized him and dragged him before the Roman governor. They said he was causing trouble in the city, but the governor refused to take sides.

'If this man had committed any crime,' he said, 'I should certainly deal with it. But as it is simply an argument about people and names, and points of your own Law, you must work it out for yourselves.'

The Greeks then took a hand. They seized Sosthenes, the new leader of the synagogue, and beat him in the Court House, but the governor still paid no attention. All this was hard for Paul. He must often have felt discouraged, and wondered if he was getting anywhere with these apparently unreliable people, and it was perhaps in such a time of discouragement that Jesus came and spoke to him one night in a dream.

'Do not be afraid,' He said, 'but go on speaking, and let no man silence you, for I Myself am with you, and no man shall lift a finger to harm you. There are many in this city who belong to Me.'

And so there were. Paul took heart. He stayed on in Corinth for eighteen months and laid firm foundations there. Priscilla and Aquila stayed with him then, and for life. Erastus, the City Treasurer, joined him too, and there were many others.

At the end of that time Paul went back to Antioch and Jerusalem to report. He sailed from Corinth taking Priscilla and Aquila with him as far as the town of Ephesus in Asia Minor where he left them to take charge. He spent a little time with the Ephesian Jews, who begged him to stay and help them, but he told them that he had to get on to Jerusalem. However, he said as he left, 'I will come back if God tells me to.'

Then he went on his way.

Apollos

WHILE Paul was away in Antioch a man called Apollos found his way to Ephesus. He was a Jew from Alexandria who had heard of John the Baptist but did not know anything that had happened since.

He went to the synagogue and started in an enterprising way to tell the Jews as much as he knew. Paul's friends Priscilla and Aquila heard him speak, and realising that he had only heard half the story, told him the rest. Once he had taken it in he said he would like to go on to Greece and tell the story there.

This Priscilla and Aquila encouraged him to do and wrote a letter to the Corinthians asking them to welcome him. Apollos seems to have been an enthusiastic, impulsive man and though he was eager to be helpful, was inclined at first to make himself the centre of the picture rather than God.

However, he knew the history of the Jews very thoroughly and everywhere he went he proved to them from the writings of the prophets that Jesus was indeed the Messiah whom they had been expecting.

He must have been a good speaker and many people came to hear him.

Paul writes to the Corinthians

PAUL did not stay long in Jerusalem and Antioch, but came back overland through Galatia to Ephesus where news reached him of trouble in Corinth. He never forgot any of the people or places he visited. They were his friends however difficult they were, and he wrote long letters to them all from different places, encouraging them, teaching them, and passing on all he had learnt himself.

Each letter took a long time to write. Try copying one out and you will see. He may have had something wrong with his eyes. Perhaps they never quite recovered from the blinding light on the Damascus road. Anyway, he generally did not write his letters himself, but dictated them to whoever was with him at the time.

Now, with the help of Timothy and Silas, he wrote one to the Corinthians.

Corinth was one of the thirteen places listed in the Acts where there were organised riots against Paul, so it was not all plain sailing for the men and women who took charge there after he left. Though there were difficulties to face from outside, they had divisions among themselves too, and Paul begins by dealing with them.

Various groups had arisen competing with each other. Apollos seems to have become the leader of one of them, and Paul writes begging them to be of one mind.

'Word has reached me,' he writes, 'that you are quarrelling and setting up different parties saying, "I belong to Paul", "I belong to Peter", "I belong to Apollos".'

Some even said 'I belong to Christ' as if He were just one leader among many.

'Who is Apollos? Who is Paul?' he asks. 'They are simply used by God. I did the planting, Apollos did the watering, but it was God who made the seed grow. So neither planter nor waterer counts, but God alone who made the seed grow.'

Then in every way Paul tries to show them God's plan for His world. 'You are God's field to be planted,' he says. 'God's house to be built. . . . You are God's temple and His spirit lives in you. So you must not boast about men. For all belongs to you. Paul, Apollos, Peter, the world, life, death, the present and the future—all belongs to you and you belong to Christ, and Christ belongs to God.'

This temple, this house of God's, he explains to them, must be kept clean, for God cannot come in where there is dirt.

It is all very well to say, 'I have the right to do as I like', but Paul says he has decided to live for other people, so that many may find what he has found.

He speaks of having gone into training like an Olympic athlete, only he looks forward to getting a much more lasting prize at the end of the race than a wreath of fading leaves. 'Why don't you run and try to win the prize?' he asks.

Then he gives a picture of the world as a body with Christ as the Head. Every part of a live and healthy body moves together, and he shows what God means our life to be, and how the world of people could move together as Christ's body on earth.

The whole world could become one body and move as one. Not with everyone doing exactly the same things, but with everyone playing the part specially given to him or her by God. He says with a twinkle in his eye (or his pen), 'Suppose your foot were to say "because I am not a hand I can't be part of the body" or your ear complained that it was not part of the whole because it is not your eye? If your whole body were an eye, what would you hear with? If your whole body were an ear, what would you smell with?

'Everybody needs everybody else. Your eye cannot say to your hand "I have no need of you". Nor can your head say it to your feet. God has put the body together in such a way that no one part is more important than another. So if one part suffers they all suffer. If one part is honoured, all the other parts share the honour.'

A little further on he shows what is going to make this body of people work together. He gives them a simple and unsentimental description of what love is and what it is not.

'Love is very patient, very kind,' he writes. 'Love knows no jealousy, makes no parade, gives itself no airs, is never rude, never selfish, never irritated, never resentful; love is never glad when others go wrong; love is gladdened by goodness, always slow to expose, always eager to believe the best, always hopeful, always patient. Love never disappears.' If you put your own name instead of 'love', Paul's meaning becomes even clearer.

Nothing but sin can destroy this body. Even dying does not kill it any more than a seed dies when it falls into the earth. It sleeps for a while and then it comes to life again.

So Paul writes almost a song of joy about the tremendous power of God which nothing can kill.

Nothing, not even death, can have power over His children. Though their bodies are buried in the earth like seeds, they will be changed into something new and glorious forever.

Though Paul felt so close to God, and Heaven was so real to him, he had his feet firmly on the ground. He was a very practical man, and as if to show that the more you were in touch with God the more business-like you had to be, he came back to a few down-to-earth arrangements about collecting money to send to Jerusalem.

'On the first day of the week,' he writes, 'let each of you put aside a sum from his weekly gains, so that the money may not have to be collected when I come.

'Perhaps I shall spend the winter with you; I hope to spend some time with you if God allows it, but I shall stay at Ephesus till Pentecost. I have many opportunities here, but many oppose me.'

He asks them to look after Timothy, who probably took the letter, and ends by saying, 'I, Paul, write this greeting with my own hand'. Then to his warm-hearted, unreliable and often ungrateful Corinthians he sends a blessing which is still said to us, perhaps without our realising to whom it was first given:

'The grace of our Lord Jesus Christ, the love of God, and the companionship of the Holy Spirit be with you all.'

'My love be with you all in Jesus Christ.'

Ephesus

AS Paul had said to the Corinthians, there was still a lot to do in Ephesus. He still stuck resolutely to giving his own people the first chance to hear what he had to say, but they were so stubborn and argumentative that after three months he moved over from the synagogue to a lecture hall in the university. This was lent to him by a professor called Tyrannus, who let Paul have it during the heat of the day when he himself was not using it.

Here Paul began to lay the foundations for a new way of life for the whole country. He covered so much ground that in two years the whole province of Asia had heard the story of how he had met Jesus, and what had happened to him through that meeting.

Ephesus itself was an important centre. Many Roman nobles sent their sons to study there. The people of the ancient world had a passionate love of learning, but in Ephesus as in Athens, though there was brilliance of mind, there was little faith. People turned then, as now, to something to hang on to when they had not found God.

In Ephesus many turned to witchcraft, which is the wrong influence of people over each other. They searched for spirits to guide them, and large numbers of books were written on how to reach these spirits and get their advice.

As the hurricane of God's power blew through men's lives, it broke the spell of witchcraft and superstition.

Books of black magic were burnt publicly. As Paul moved about among them, many were healed of illnesses both of mind and body, and a great tide of new life began to rise.

Paul's thoughts began to turn to his friends in Macedonia. He sent Timothy on ahead with Erastus, the City Treasurer of Corinth, to prepare for his coming. Just as he was leaving another storm blew up. The fact that so many people were turning to him meant that certain traders in Ephesus had begun to lose money.

Ephesus was the headquarters of the worship of the goddess Diana, and the chief industry of the city was making silver models of this goddess to sell to visitors. Because of Paul's teaching, interest in Diana began to die down, and so did the trade in silver models.

This led to another tremendous uproar. It was started by a silversmith called Demetrius. He gathered the other smiths together, and said to them, 'You know that we have to make our living by our work. Now this man Paul comes along, not only here, but in many other cities, and says that gods made with hands are not gods at all. This is bad for trade and an insult to the great goddess Diana, whom we and the whole world worship.'

The workers were glad to have someone to blame, and shouting 'Great Diana of the Ephesians', they surged through the city looking for a victim. They did not find Paul, but seized on two of his Greek friends, Gaius and Aristarchus, and dragged them to the great open-air theatre which was the public meeting place.

When Paul heard of this he wanted to go into the theatre and speak to the crowd, but certain of the city leaders felt it would be too dangerous. There was a scene of fearful confusion. Some people were shouting one thing and some another. Most of them had no idea why they had come,

or what the fuss was all about, but they joined in just the same.

After a while a man called Alexander tried to speak to the crowd, but when they realised that he was a Jew, like Paul, a great roar went up. They stood there shouting, 'Great is Diana of the Ephesians! Great is Diana of the Ephesians!' for two hours without stopping.

By that time most of them were simply shouting for the sake of shouting, and the Town Clerk came and took charge.

He quieted the mob and got their attention. Then he said, 'Everybody knows that the city of Ephesus worships Diana. There is no need to shout about it. These men have done nothing wrong, and if they

had, the proper course would be to bring them before the magistrates. As it is we are all likely to get into trouble for causing this riot. There is not a single reason we can give for this unruly meeting.' This brought the Ephesians to their senses, and slightly sobered they went home.

It was hard for Paul. Courageous as ever, he pursued his earlier plan of going on to Macedonia, but he was sick at heart. He had been three years in Ephesus, and was deeply saddened by the Ephesians having apparently turned against all he had taught them during those years. It was as if his own children had knifed him, and he was hurt and discouraged as he set off towards Greece, stopping at Troas on the way. Troas was where he had first met Luke. This time he hoped to meet his friend Titus, the Greek, who had gone with him to the Conference at Jerusalem some years earlier. But Titus had not arrived. So after waiting in vain for some days, Paul moved on to Philippi.

Here he wrote again to the Corinthians telling them of his distress over all that had happened to him in Asia. 'I was crushed,' he writes, 'crushed far more than I could stand, so much that I despaired even of life.'

However, to his great joy, Titus turned up in Philippi, having come from Corinth with more heartening news. Evidently the Corinthians had mended their ways, and this comforted Paul after all he had been through with the Ephesians. The very fact that the Corinthians were such a troublesome lot seems to have endeared them to him, and he was not too proud to tell them when he was in difficulties himself. At the same time he never hesitated to give them a piece of his mind if he felt they needed it.

He poured out his heart to them, and his life for them. Besides thanking, encouraging and teaching them, he told them simply what he had had to face in his fight to make God's Plan the plan for nations.

Often at the point of death, beaten five times by the Jews, and three times by the Romans. Stoned once, ship-wrecked three times, adrift at sea for a day and a night. His life was constantly in danger, he says, from rivers and robbers, from Jews and Gentiles, in towns in deserts and at sea. Sometimes betrayed by false friends, he went through sleepless nights, hunger and thirst; often starving, cold and poorly clad.

Through all this ran his ceaseless thought and care for the men and women who had been entrusted to him. Many of them, including the Corinthians themselves, did not understand what he was doing, and accused him of boasting. But he says he would never have gone through all this on his own account, and that he certainly has nothing to boast of, unless they count being constantly knocked about and not feeling at all well most of the time.

For God, says Paul, has given him something which he calls 'a thorn in the flesh' to stop him from ever getting puffed up. This was possibly the trouble he had with his eyes, or some other weakness. It meant that he could never rely on how he was feeling, but always had to trust God for strength to carry him through.

So in his own weakness but in God's strength he went on to Corinth.

Paul writes to the Romans

IT was about the year 56. For the third time Paul was in Corinth, where he had first met Priscilla and Aquila. Partly through them, and partly through others, he knew a lot about what was going on in Rome. He knew the names of many people there and the thought of reaching Rome was always with him. He began to prepare for his going by writing to the men and women in the city whom he already knew by name.

The emperor at that time was Nero, who later organised the torture and murder of thousands of Christians. This persecution had not yet started, but there were signs of what lay ahead. The emperor himself was vain, cruel and twisted. Everyone jostled for power, and nobody minded how they got it. Murder, bribery, divorce and every kind of cruelty and self-indulgence were part of the Roman way of life, so that after a while people who lived differently could hardly fail to be noticed.

It was to these men and women that Paul wrote, warning them of what happened to those who turned away from God and His standards. First he says how much he wants to see them, because the world has abandoned God and is in a dangerous plight. When men stop putting God first, they are bound to put themselves first, and 'as they do not choose to know God', he writes, 'God lets them go the way their twisted minds take them'.

Paul then describes people who have forsaken God. They use their bodies as the only link with other people, as animals do. It leads to murder, lying and envy. Such people hate God. They become proud and scornful, 'inventors of evil', he says, 'disobedient to their parents'.

He deals with what today is called homosexuality as part of what men turn to when they turn away from God. They understand nothing, they break their promises, have no real love for anyone, and become hard and unmerciful. In time they come to enjoy the most horrible things, and the gifts God could and would give them have no meaning for them.

Then Paul goes on to say that, bad as people can be, Jesus took the wickedness of the world upon Himself when He died. Our sin killed His body, so that it need not kill us. Just as Jesus came to life again, so can we, if we let Jesus have all the rotten things that are choking us to death.

These things can die as Jesus died, and we can come to life again as He did.

'It is a battle to choose the right way to go,' says Paul. 'I know, because I keep finding myself wanting to do wrong things even though I know I ought not to. But the law of the spirit of life in Jesus Christ makes me free from the law of sin and death.'

'Nothing,' he says later, 'can separate us from the love of Christ, neither trouble nor distress, nor famine nor loss, nor danger nor war. In all these things we are more than conquerors through Him that loved us.'

It was a message the Christians in Rome were soon going to need as a reality. They were going to need strength from somewhere outside themselves, if they were not going to take the easy way and go with the tide. Paul knew that it was much easier to try to keep in with people, and do what everyone else was doing, than to make a stand. So in a city full of sex and vice, he tells the Romans to keep their bodies like a living sacrifice.

This was an interesting idea, because an animal that was sacrificed had to be perfect, with no disease or impurity in it. Paul sees living people who have sacrificed their own selfishness as a more reasonable gift to God. They do not have to accept the standard of the world outside. They can be transformed from inside. They can have new minds which will show them what God really wants.

Then he moves to a few practical points about his own plans, in his usual matter-of-fact way.

'I hope to come to you on my way to Spain,' he says, 'but I have to go to Jerusalem first. The people of Macedonia and Achaia (north and south Greece) have collected money for our friends in Jerusalem, and I shall have to take it to them.'

He ends with special greetings to people whose names he knows. Priscilla and Aquila had evidently gone back to Rome, and Paul speaks with gratitude of a time when they had risked their lives to save his. He mentions more than twenty other people by name, and sends them messages from the men who were with him. Timothy was one. So was Erastus, the City Treasurer of Corinth, who had been with him in Ephesus. You get the picture of a man who deeply cared for people and never forgot anyone.

His letter ends by commending them all to God. Then he gave it to some traveller going to Rome, where it was read aloud and treasured for all time, and that is why we can still read it today.

But for the moment Paul himself turned his footsteps towards Jerusalem.

The last journey to Jerusalem

PAUL wrote his letter to the Romans from Corinth during his last three months' visit to Greece, about 57 or 58. Before reaching Corinth he had been to see all his old friends in Philippi, Berea and Thessalonica, because he knew that he would never see them again. He was in constant danger. In fact, a plot on his life was discovered just as he was about to start back to the mainland again by sea, but he had a group of seven determined men travelling with him by that time. Among them was the faithful Timothy.

When the plot came to light, these men decided to carry on with the plan of going by sea, while Paul, and Luke who had rejoined the party, slipped off quietly by land.

'They went on ahead', writes Luke, 'and waited for us at Troas.'

In this way, Paul gave his enemies the slip, as no one noticed he was not in the main group. He and Luke spent a week at Troas after meeting the rest of the party who had gone by sea, but all the time Paul had been feeling more and more strongly that he must get back to Jerusalem. He wanted to be there for Pentecost, but to go in such a way that he could say good-bye to his friends in Asia.

So, much as he wanted to press on, he went by ship from town to town along the Asian coast to see them. As Ephesus was some way inland he sent a message to the Ephesian elders asking them to come and meet him at Miletus, the nearest sea-port.

They did not know when he left after the riot, that he would never come back. For twenty years he had been travelling up and down all over Greece and the provinces of Asia Minor. No matter what he went through he always re-appeared. It was unthinkable to them that there should be a last time. But the last time had come and gone without their realising it. His oldest friends, who must have hoped that they would be able to make Paul's next visit more successful than the last, came post haste to Miletus, when they got his message.

There by the sea he gathered them together and spoke lovingly to them. 'You know how I have lived among you in Asia all these years,' he said, 'serving God humbly, and often with tears because of the many plots against me. I have kept nothing back from you, but have taught in public and from house to house. I have spoken to the Jews and to the Greeks about how to change and have faith. Now I am sent by the Holy Spirit to Jerusalem. He keeps telling me that chains and difficulties are awaiting me. But none of this troubles me because I do not value my own life provided I can cheerfully finish the course which God has laid down for me.

'And now as I know that you will never see me again, I want to put on record that no one has met his death through me, and I have not hesitated to tell you all that God has told me. From now on, you must look after others as I have looked after you, for after I have left you, men will come in among you like wolves among sheep. They will take many of you away from what I have taught you. So you must watch and remember how I warned you, all through these last three years, of what lay ahead.'

Then he told them that it was God Himself who would care for them. He, Paul, had worked to support himself and them, so as to show them the way to care for others, and he reminded them of how Jesus had said that it was better to give than to get.

After that he prayed with them, and they wept bitterly at the thought of not seeing him again. Then they went sadly to the ship to see him off. It was a coasting vessel which called at several places and finally came to Tyre in Syria. Here the cargo was unloaded, and Paul and his party had to wait a week for another ship.

His friends in Tyre knew what he would be up against in Jerusalem, and warned him not to go; but his mind was made up.

So, as at Miletus, they went down to the shore to see him off. Whole families came with their children. They saw the little old man who never thought of himself sail out of their lives. With him went his faithful companions.

The next port was Caesarea in country over which Jesus Himself had travelled. Here Paul stayed with Philip, the man who had baptised the Ethiopian Treasurer. Here, too, he again met the prophet Agabus who had foretold the famine in Jerusalem many years earlier.

Agabus took Paul's belt and tied his own hands with it saying, 'The Holy Spirit says this, "The man to whom this girdle belongs will be bound by the Jews in Jerusalem, and handed over to the Gentiles."'

On hearing this, Paul's friends broke into loud lamentations, but the old warrior hushed them.

'Why do you weep and break my heart?' he asked. 'I am quite ready not only to be bound, but to die for Jesus at Jerusalem.'

Even Luke joined in begging him not to go, but writing of it later, he said, 'When he would not be persuaded we stopped, and said "God's will must be done." '

So this fearless and determined little group, drawn from the cities of Greece and Asia Minor, picked up their luggage and went on. Their names appear later in Paul's letters. Sopater of Berea, Aristarchus and Secundus of Thessalonica. Gaius of Derbe and Timothy from Lystra. Tychicus and Trophimus from Asia (probably Ephesus).

All these with Paul and Luke now set off, as Jesus had done before them, for Jerusalem.

The Arrest

A CYPRIOT whom they had known in the early days put them up in Jerusalem, and the next day they went to see James and the other leaders to report.

These men were all delighted with the progress among the Jews, but were less satisfied with Paul's attitude to the Law.

'See, brother,' they said, 'there are thousands of Jews here now for the feast. They all keep the Law faithfully. Now they hear that you are giving the Gentiles the impression that the Law is not important. In order to set their minds at rest, we suggest that you should take a special vow in the Temple with four poor men who cannot afford to come up without help. If you take this vow with them and pay their expenses, everyone will see that you care for the poor and keep the Law and are still a good Jew.'

It was one of those suggestions which sound reasonable enough, and Paul, for whatever reason, agreed to do it. However, as it turned out, this narrow insistence by the Jewish leaders on keeping up appearances did not lead him out of trouble, but straight into it.

The vow was one that had been taken by John the Baptist. It meant leading a disciplined life in various ways, and there was nothing wrong with it. It also meant spending a week in the Temple saying special prayers.

So Paul left the party who had travelled from Asia with him, and went to the Temple. Other Jews from Asia, among them many of his old enemies from Ephesus, had also come up for Pentecost. They started a rumour that Trophimus the Greek, whom they had seen with Paul, had gone in too. As he was a Gentile this was not allowed, and they went round working the other Asian Jews into a state of fury about Paul having broken the Law.

Incidentally, anyone who had taken the trouble to go and look would have seen that Trophimus was not in the Temple with Paul, but nobody bothered to find out what was true and what was not.

By the end of the week of prayer, the Jews from Asia had collected enough support to storm down to the Temple in a mass. They burst in and seized Paul, shouting, 'Here is the man who is teaching everyone not to obey the law of Moses.' Then they dragged him out of the Temple.

The priests immediately shut the doors so that he could not get in again, putting him at the mercy of an infuriated and senseless mob. They were about to kill him when the officer in charge of the Temple appeared. The confusion was so great that he had been told the whole city was rioting, and had brought soldiers to restore order.

When the ringleaders saw the troops coming, they stopped beating Paul. The officer, Claudius Lysias, had him put in chains. By Roman law whatever a man had done, he had to have a fair trial.

Even so, the soldiers had to carry Paul to save him from the mob. They cried, 'Kill him, kill him,' but when Chief Captain Lysias tried to find out why, some shouted one thing and some another, so that he could make neither head nor tail of it.

He told the soldiers to take Paul into the barracks. At the top of the

steps that led into the fortress, Paul turned to him and said in Greek, 'May I speak to you?' As this was a language used by educated men, the captain was surprised to hear his prisoner speaking it.

'So you know Greek, do you?' he said. 'Aren't you the Egyptian who started a riot here not long ago?'

'I am a Jew,' replied Paul. 'I am a man of Tarsus, and Tarsus is no mean city. Will you let me speak to the people?'

The captain gave his permission, and Paul stepped forward. He signed to the crowd to be quiet, and a great silence fell on them all. Paul started to talk to them, this time in Hebrew, their own language. Once again he told the story of how he had met Jesus on the way to Damascus, after he had watched Stephen being put to death.

Everyone listened quietly up to this point, but then Paul went on to say that Jesus had sent him to the Gentiles.

At this, the shouting broke out again.

'Away with him. He is not fit to live,' cried the crowd, tearing off their clothes, and throwing dust into the air.

It made the captain think there must be some reason for these strong feelings, and he decided to have Paul flogged to make him confess what he had done to stir up all this trouble.

But once more there was a surprise in store for him. When Paul saw what the soldiers were going to do, he said, 'Are you allowed to beat a Roman citizen who has not been found guilty?'

One of them reported this to the captain, who was considerably shaken.

'Are you a Roman citizen?' he asked.

'Yes,' answered Paul.

'It cost me a lot of money to become a citizen,' said the captain.

'But I was born free,' said Paul.

There was a system of buying citizenship, which was evidently what Lysias had done, but Paul inherited his freedom from his father. So he was even more firmly a citizen than the man who had thought of having him flogged.

By this time, Claudius Lysias had decided that more needed to be known about this remarkable man who had landed in his charge. He ordered the irons to be taken off him, and took him next day before a council of the chief priests.

There were two parties in the Council, the Pharisees and the Sadducees. The Sadducees did not believe in angels or spirits, or in the Holy Spirit. They did not believe in life after death either, but the Pharisees believed in both.

So when Paul started to speak of Jesus having risen from the dead, there was a great uproar from the Sadducees who said it was all nonsense. The Pharisees, on the other hand, though they disagreed with Paul about many things, also disagreed violently with the Sadducees. In next to no time a fierce argument had broken out.

Finally, some of the Pharisees said, 'We find nothing wrong with this man. Suppose some angel or spirit really has spoken to him?'

The feeling on both sides then ran so high that Captain Lysias feared that Paul would be torn to pieces between them. Nor was anything being settled, so he ordered his men to rescue Paul and take him back to the barracks.

That night Jesus again stood by Paul and said, 'Take heart. For as you have spoken bravely for Me in Jerusalem, so you must go and speak for Me in Rome.'

Paul goes before Governors

ALTHOUGH Paul escaped harm for the time being, certain Jews banded together and swore not to eat or drink till they had killed him. Over forty of them made this plan, but they needed help to carry it out.

So they sent to the chief priests and suggested a trick to trap Paul.

'Tell the officer in charge,' they said, 'that you want to question the prisoner further. Then Paul will be brought out of the barracks, and we shall be ready to kill him on the way to see you.'

Fortunately, Paul's nephew heard of the plot, and told his uncle. Paul sent him straight to Captain Lysias.

By this time Lysias was convinced that whatever Paul had done, the priests and the Jews were up to no good. He told Paul's nephew to keep quiet and tell no one that he had been to see him. Then he sat down and wrote a letter to the Roman governor.

'This man had been seized by the Jews,' he wrote, 'and was about to be murdered by them when I arrived with my troops and rescued him. I found that he was a Roman citizen, and wanted to know what the charge was against him. So I had him brought before their council, and found he was accused of questions of their own laws. There was no charge which deserved either death or imprisonment.

Now, however, I have had private information of a plot against his life, so I am sending him to you at once. At the same time I have told his accusers that they must charge him in front of you.'

Lysias then ordered two hundred men to be ready that night to take Paul with the letter to Caesarea. He also ordered seventy horsemen, two hundred spearmen, and a horse for Paul himself to carry him safely to Felix, the governor.

They started at nine o'clock and rode through the night. The soldiers took Paul to the governor, delivered the letter, and went back to Jerusalem. Felix read the letter, and told Paul he would have to wait till his accusers arrived. Then both sides would be heard. In the meantime Paul was kept as a prisoner in the King's Palace.

Five days later Ananias, the High Priest, arrived with some of the elders and a lawyer, and the trial began.

The lawyer began by flattering Felix. He said how grateful they all were to the most noble Felix for his wise rule, which had so wonderfully kept the peace. Unfortunately they now had a most troublesome fellow before them, who was causing disturbances all over the world. He was a leader of the Nazarenes (or followers of Jesus of Nazareth). He had dishonoured the Temple, and when the Jews had tried to take him and judge him according to their laws, Captain Lysias had removed him by force.

Paul was then asked what he had to say. He replied that he had been quietly praying in the Temple when a great mob set on him.

'There was no mob', he said, 'and no disturbance until these Jews from Asia came, and they should have come and told you first if they had anything against me. What is being called in question is my belief that Jesus is still alive.'

Now Felix, though he was the governor, did not come from an influential family. He was the son of a freed slave. He was a bully to weaker people and anxious to keep in with stronger ones. His wife,

Drusilla, was the daughter of Herod who had put Peter in prison and tried to have himself proclaimed a god. She had been married to an Arabian puppet king and Felix had felt strong enough to take her away from him.

He knew something of the way of life that Paul stood for, but had never tried to live it himself. He did not know what support Paul had, and he wanted to keep in with everyone. He wanted to please the Romans. He wanted to please the Jews. He also was quite ready to find a way of letting Paul off.

As he could not do all these things at once, he made no decision. He gave orders for Paul to be kept in prison, but to be well treated. His friends could visit him and bring him anything he needed.

Some days later Felix and Drusilla sent for Paul and questioned him about what he believed in. They may have felt that there was something missing in their own lives which Paul's faith might be able to fill.

However, Paul talked of very down-to-earth matters like morals and self-control and judgment, and Felix realised that he would have to do more than listen if he was going to find a faith. It made him feel uncomfortable and after a while he said, 'You may go now. When I find a convenient moment I will send for you again.'

And Paul was taken away.

Felix did find some convenient moments later, but the talks never got far. He would have liked to let Paul go, but did not dare to. He kept hoping that in the course of conversation Paul would suggest buying his way out, but he never did. He offered the governor no money. He just offered him the chance to choose a new way of living.

This chance Felix never took. He was so anxious to please everyone, including himself, that he ended by doing nothing. So the talks went on at intervals for two years, until at the end of that time he was recalled and another governor was appointed.

Before he left he made a last attempt to please the Jews, and left Paul in prison.

The new governor was called Festus. The first thing he did was to spend three days in Caesarea, finding out about his new work. He heard that a Jew called Paul had been in prison for two years. There seemed to be no reason for it, so when he went to Jerusalem, he decided to find out why.

This was the chance the chief priests and the Council had been waiting for. They applied to the new governor to have Paul tried legally, as they said, at Jerusalem. What they did not say was that they had once more arranged to have Paul killed on the way, so that he would never reach Jerusalem at all.

But Festus was a Roman. He knew the way to hold trials, and may also have had his suspicions about the whole affair. He said that Paul would be kept at Caesarea, and that the trial would be there.

'Then,' he said, 'any of you who can prove that this man has done wrong can come and present your case.'

And before Kings

TEN days later Festus came back to Caesarea bringing some of the leading Jews from Jerusalem, and the next day he had Paul brought before him.

The Jews laid their charges, but were not able to prove any of them.

Paul, when he was asked to speak, simply answered, 'I have done nothing against the Jewish Law, nor against the Temple, nor against Caesar.' So there it was again. The Jews said he had done wrong. Paul said he had done nothing wrong. Festus did not know enough about the Jewish Law to know which was true. Also, like Felix, he wanted to please the Jews. He was not sure what to do next.

So he said, 'Are you willing to go to Jerusalem to be tried there before me?' However, by this time Paul felt it had all gone on long enough. Also, he wanted to get to Rome, not stay for ever in Caesarea. So he did something which surprised them all.

'I am standing before Caesar's judgment seat,' he said, 'and that is where I should be tried. I have done the Jews no wrong, as you know very well. If I had done anything deserving of death I would not refuse to die, but if no one can prove any of these things, then no one can sentence me. I appeal to Caesar.'

Any Roman citizen had the right to go straight to the emperor if he felt he was not being fairly treated, and once he had asked to be sent to Caesar he had to go.

Festus was in a difficulty, because he could give no reason for sending him, and a written accusation was supposed to go with any prisoner sent to Rome.

He felt in need of advice. So when a few days later Agrippa, the Jewish king of Caesarea, with his sister Bernice, came on a state visit, Festus decided to consult him.

The men who were called kings at this time were not like David and Solomon and the old kings of Israel and Judah. They were Jews, it is true; but while the kings in those days had been rulers of a free nation which at any rate felt it ought to serve God, these new kings frankly served the Romans. They were appointed by them, and were more anxious to please Caesar than to please God.

Agrippa was well able to understand what the dispute between Paul and the priests was about. He, too, was one of the Herod family. His great grandfather Herod had given the order to kill the children after Jesus was born. His uncle Herod was the man who had John the Baptist beheaded, and had sent Jesus to Pilate. His father Herod was also the father of Drusilla, the wife of Felix. For four generations his family had been faced with the Way of the Cross and had turned away from it. When he and Bernice arrived, Festus explained the position to them.

'I have a man here,' he said, 'who was left in prison by Felix. The chief priests and elders of the Jews want a judgment given against him, but I told them that it was not the Roman way to condemn a man without a trial. It all seems to be about a certain Jesus who has died, but who Paul says is still alive. I did not feel able to decide, and I asked Paul if he were willing to go to Jerusalem to be tried, but he has asked to be sent to Caesar. So I am keeping him here until such time as I can send him to Rome.'

'I have been wanting to hear this man myself,' said Agrippa.

'Then,' replied Festus, 'you shall hear him tomorrow,' and the next day Paul was brought before the king and Bernice.

Festus explained the situation to them and to officers of the army and leading citizens who had come with them. He ended by saying, 'So I have brought Paul before you all, and especially before you, King Agrippa, for it seems ridiculous to send a prisoner before the emperor without saying what crimes he has committed.'

After listening carefully, Agrippa said to Paul, 'You may speak for yourself.'

Then, as he had so often done before, Paul told the story of his meeting with Jesus, and of how bitterly he had once fought against Him. He told them of how Jesus had said to him, 'You are chosen to be My servant to tell people of what you have seen today. I will keep

you safe both from your own people and from the Gentiles, to whom I now send you. I send you to open their eyes, to turn them from darkness to light, from the power of Satan to God Himself, so that they may be forgiven and take their place with all those who are made holy by their faith in Me.'

'After that, King Agrippa,' said Paul, 'I could not disobey the heavenly vision. I went everywhere, to the Jews and to the Gentiles telling men that they could change and turn to God. This is why the Jews seized me in the Temple, and tried to kill me. But I stand here to say what Moses and all the Prophets said, which was that Jesus would be killed and come back to life, and take His message to the Jews and to the Gentiles.'

Paul stopped speaking and Festus, who had not heard the story before, said, 'You are crazy, Paul, all your learning has driven you mad.'

'No,' replied Paul. 'I am not mad. It is all true. The king knows about it. None of these things were done in secret.'

Then turning to the king, he said, 'King Agrippa, do you believe the Prophets? But I know that you believe them.'

It was a hard question for the king to answer. As a Jew, the

answer was 'Yes', and yet so many of the Jews were against Paul that Agrippa dared not side with him. Festus obviously did not believe a word of what Paul had said, and for Agrippa to say he did believe it might make him look silly in front of the governor.

Agrippa could not say yes. He could not say no. Many people have written about what they thought went on in his mind. What he said at last was, 'You almost persuade me to be a Christian.'

And Paul knew that the king, like so many others, did not have the courage to decide. He also knew that though he was a prisoner in chains he was much freer than the men who were judging him.

'I wish,' he said, 'that all of you were not "almost" but "exactly" like me.'

Then he looked down at his hands, and perhaps gave a little smile and added, 'except, of course, for these chains.'

Everyone then got up rather hurriedly, but they were still no nearer to deciding what his crime was. The king, with Bernice and Festus and the rest of the court, moved away to talk it over together. They did not choose to accept the life that Paul was offering them, but they were quite clear that he had done nothing to deserve a punishment.

'In fact,' said Agrippa to Festus, 'if he had not appealed to Caesar we could have let him go.'

By that time they may have been wishing they had done so long ago, but they had missed their chance. They were going to have to send a prisoner to the emperor with no reasonable explanation, which might make them both look rather silly.

As for Paul, his greatest wish had been granted. He was going to Rome.

The voyage to Rome

PAUL was going to Rome. It was not the way he would have chosen, left to himself, but it had one advantage, which was that his passage was paid by the government.

It was decided that he should travel with some other prisoners in charge of a centurion called Julius. With him went the Thessalonian Aristarchus. Luke the doctor went too.

Paul was no longer a young man. Nearly thirty years had passed since Jesus had stopped him on the Damascus road. His thorn in the flesh, whatever it was, never stopped him from doing what God told him to do. It remained as a constant test of whether he would put his own health and comfort first, or God's will.

Anyway, we can imagine the faithful Luke deciding to go with him and look after him.

They set sail one autumn day. The ship called at different ports and at one of them, Julius, who was a kindly man, allowed Paul and his party to go ashore and visit their friends.

After a while they changed ships and went on slowly as the autumn

winds were blowing hard, so that they only just managed to reach the island of Crete.

Paul pointed out to the centurion that if they went on once the winter gales had started the ship might be lost with everyone on board. He suggested that they might spend the winter in a sheltered port and sail again in the spring.

The centurion consulted the captain of the ship, who thought he knew better and said that there was no danger. So they set off once more.

But before long a violent gale swept down on the ship, which was a good deal smaller than the ones which now cross the English Channel. It was no good trying to steer and the sailors had to let her be blown along by the wind. The water came pouring in and, to lighten the ship, part of the cargo was thrown overboard. Three days later the spare ropes and masts and sails were thrown overboard too. And still the storm went on.

For two weeks the sun neither showed by day nor the stars at night, and the crew began to think there was no hope of being saved.

But one night God spoke to Paul and told him that he was going to reach Rome. The men would be saved but the ship would be lost, and Paul heartened them with this news next day.

Two weeks later they found themselves nearing an island. To try and save the ship, the sailors let down anchors. It was night so they prayed and waited for the dawn. They had decided to launch a life-boat as soon as it was light, and escape unseen.

Once more Paul was on the spot, and warned Julius. He knew that if the sailors ran away no one could be saved, because they were the only men who knew how to handle the ship.

When the soldiers heard of this, they cut the ropes that held the boat and it drifted away. So now they were all going to have to stick together whether they liked it or not.

It was still dark and Paul took charge of the situation, prisoner though he was. No one had eaten properly for nearly a fortnight, so he found some bread and when he had thanked God, he broke it and handed it round.

The exhausted men began to recover some strength and when they had eaten they threw overboard the last of the cargo, which was corn.

When dawn broke, they saw a bay with a sandy shore and decided to run the ship on to the beach.

Unfortunately, they hit a sandbank on the way and went aground. The bow of the ship was stuck in the sand and the waves breaking against the stern broke her in half.

The soldiers then thought they should kill all the prisoners in case they should swim ashore and escape, but that would have included Paul. He had just saved all their lives, so Julius gave orders for each man to save himself in any way he could. There were two hundred and seventy-six men altogether. Some swam ashore, and others followed clinging to planks and anything they could get hold of. So it came true that everyone landed in safety.

This island is what we today call Malta and there is still a bay there called St. Paul's Bay.

The shipwrecked party did not try again to force their way through the winter storms, but stayed in Malta for three months. Paul became much loved by the islanders and he healed many who were ill.

When spring came they set sail once more in another ship and the grateful islanders brought them presents as they left.

With a soft wind blowing from the south, in less than a week they reached the town of Puteoli in Italy, just south of Rome.

Here they were met by a group of Christians who asked Paul and Luke to spend a week with them.

When it was over, they started on foot for the great city Paul had so long dreamed of reaching.

Rome

S O they reached Rome.
The men and women to whom Paul had written from Corinth came out from the city to meet him. For the first time he saw the faces of those whose names he knew so well.

He was not put in prison, because there was still no charge against him. On the other hand he could not be set free because he was awaiting trial, though what he was to be tried for was not quite clear. He lived in what is described as a hired house, for two years, but to make it plain that he was still a prisoner, he was chained night and day to a soldier.

A building of this period has been unearthed recently which may have been where Paul lived. It is a grain-store, consisting of a long barn with small store houses along the outer walls.

The smaller divisions held the corn, and it was taken from them to the central hall to be sold. If one of these had been turned into a small house for Paul he could have used the big barn when he needed more space to meet people and talk to them.

He was allowed to have visitors, and apart from being chained to the soldier, was free to move about and have people in to see him. It was a wonderful opportunity to do what he had come to Rome to do, namely, to spread his ideas across the empire, and build a force inside the capital itself. Many of his old friends and fellow-fighters evidently joined him. Timothy certainly did, for we find him there still writing Paul's letters.

Men in a later age who were put in prison, or exiled, for their revolutionary ideas, spent the time writing down what they believed for the world to read. They wrote clear and well-thought-out plans for bringing the world under the rule of one class or one race.

Paul wrote of how the world could be ruled by God through men and women who obeyed Him.

Through his little house, whatever it was like, men came and went. They took Paul's messages and training manuals in the form of letters all over Greece and Asia Minor, where they were read and copied. They were handed on to the people of that time, and have been read by millions ever since.

Because his work was based on people, he nearly always put in little personal touches, either about the ones who were with him, or those to whom he was writing.

In his letter to the Colossians, whom incidentally he had never met, he let them know who was with him in Rome by sending greetings from them all.

They included Mark, who had re-enlisted and come back; also Aristarchus, Luke, Timothy and various others.

This letter was probably taken to Colosse by a runaway slave called Onesimus, who had stolen from his master and then escaped to Rome. Paul dealt with Onesimus tenderly but firmly, and sent him back to put things straight with his master. He also wrote to the master, Philemon, asking him to forgive Onesimus, and accept him not just as a slave, but as a friend and fellow-fighter.

Again those who signed the letter were Mark, Luke and Aristarchus, with Timothy acting as secretary. Another man, Demas, signed, but backed out later when things got difficult, and left.

Paul.was a practical man, and as there was a messenger going back to Turkey and Syria, he took the opportunity of giving him a batch of letters to leave at various places on the way, Colosse being the farthest off.

So he wrote to the Ephesians. It was probably a round robin to go

to all the other centres. He also wrote to the Philippians who had evidently sent him either food or money, by a Colossian called Epaphras, who was passing through on his way to Rome.

He thanked the Philippians for their care of him, but among other things also urged them to deal with two quarrelling women called Euodias and Syntyche. He knew that difficult women can wreck any situation, and to Paul nothing was too unimportant to mention.

He knew that big doors swing on little hinges, and while he wrote about the depth and greatness of God's Plan, he also showed what in human nature continually holds it up. He struck at what was, and is, wrong with the world. He said that it was sin, that is to say, the idea that 'I am at the centre of the picture'.

There were many things wrong with society, then as now— slavery, oppression, imperialism and colonialism. Paul's teaching tackled the very root of all these evils. He dealt with the greediness, ambition and rottenness of the people who were part of it. He knew that you can't make a good omelette out of bad eggs, and that only new people can make a new world.

* * *

Paul lived in his hired house from about the years 61 to 63 and was left in peace. He had done nothing worthy of punishment as far as the Romans were concerned. He was a Jew who had disagreed with some other Jews, and it was not the concern of the Romans until they had some more information about it.

Luke only says that he was there for two years, and then the story stops quite suddenly.

Paul was probably put on trial, but was released. Perhaps whatever evidence was produced was not convincing, which was just as well, because Paul writing later to Timothy says, 'At my first defence no man stood by me. I pray that it will not be held against them.' He also says that he was delivered from the lion's mouth, which sounds as if he had been tried and let off.

Paul's teaching and way of life penetrated quietly but persistently all through Rome, reaching right into Caesar's household. The handful of men and women who had come out of the city to meet Paul were growing into an army.

But for the moment the Roman authorities did not realise how large it had become. No one seems to have bothered about Paul getting more people into what appeared to be just another Jewish group.

At some point Peter came to Rome too. He and the other older apostles no longer made Jerusalem their headquarters. Though Peter longed for his own people to see what was so clear to him, not many of them did, and he seems to have moved to Antioch, and from there to Rome.

Some say that Paul took the opportunity in his year of freedom to go to Spain, and that he then made one last visit to his friends in Asia, taking Timothy and others with him.

Then in the year 64 there was a terrible fire in Rome. No one knows who started it. Some said it was the emperor himself, but as no one could accuse him, the police looked round for someone else to blame.

Could it be all these Christians? The emperor Nero had ordered everyone to say that he was a god, and this the Christians always refused to do, though they were quite prepared to obey him in other matters. It made them convenient targets for blame, and it began to be said that they had started the fire.

The rumour was spread around that they were undercover revolutionaries. This in a way was true, though it was not the kind of revolution the government thought. As a result, many of Paul's courageous band were rounded up and put to death in horrible ways.

Paul, too, was arrested again, and taken back to prison. Only Luke went with him. Timothy and some of the others were left to hold the fort in Ephesus.

Back in Rome, this time Paul had no hired house. He was thrown into the lower dungeon of the Mamertine Prison, which was really a cave below the main prison. People could only be put into it by lowering them through a hole in the floor. It was dark and wet and cold, but he still had Luke with him and was able to write letters.

It is said that over a hundred jailers enlisted in Paul's revolution while he was there. The governor had to keep replacing them in the hope that each new one would be less likely to change than the last. Perhaps these jailers found a way for the letters to be written and taken out. People certainly came to see him even there.

In the course of the police round-up Peter was arrested too, and today guides point out the pillar to which he and Paul were chained. But Paul knew that the end was coming, and he wrote a moving final letter to Timothy, who was still in Asia.

'For I am now ready to be offered', he writes, 'and the time of my departure is at hand. I have fought a good fight. I have finished the race. I have kept the faith.'

Then he asks Timothy to come as soon as possible.

'Do your best to come to me soon', he writes. 'Demas, having loved this present world, has left me and gone to Thessalonica . . . only Luke is with me. When you come, pick up Mark and bring him with you. . . . And please bring the cloak I left at Troas with Carpus, and the books, especially the manuscripts.'

He must have felt the need of his cloak in the piercing cold of the lower dungeon.

He was a courageous fighter, thinker and statesman. In his letters Paul writes to the men and women of his own day, and also to all of us, showing the way to find strength and courage and a plan to win the world for God.

He speaks of the fight we are all in. He says, 'We are up against the power that controls this dark world . . . therefore you must wear the whole armour of God.' He speaks of the belt of truth, the breastplate of living straight, and the shoes of peace. Not peace at any price, but the peace that comes when people become different. He saw people as soldiers attacking what is wrong, with the sword of the Spirit, and then when things get difficult, 'above all', he says, 'you will need the shield of faith'.

He was at peace, for he knew he had done what he had been told to do, and he waited quietly for the last step.

One morning about the year 67 or 68, soldiers came and fetched him from prison. They took him down the Ostian Way, to be beheaded. To be beheaded rather than crucified was his last privilege as a Roman citizen. Three springs of water sprang up by the milestone of Aquae Silviae where it is said his head fell. They have been flowing ever since like the stream of new life which Paul left behind him.

Peter

PETER worked with Paul in Rome, though there are no written records of his stay there. By the time he arrived it was probably no longer possible or safe to keep records, but many stories are told of how he lived among the persecuted Christians.

One tradition is that when they saw that many of them were going to be killed they persuaded Peter to escape. He would be more use alive than dead, they argued. He was an old man too, and had been through so much suffering that they wanted to spare him any more.

Peter himself had tried to say this to Jesus over thirty years earlier. In the end he agreed to go, and set off down the Appian Way.

The story goes that, as he walked away from Rome, he suddenly came face to face with Jesus, going towards it. 'Where are you going, Lord?' asked Peter. 'I am going to be crucified again instead of you,' replied Jesus.

Peter then saw that he was running away as he had done once before, and he turned back. Soon afterwards he was arrested, and condemned to death.

He was not a Roman citizen like Paul, and he was sentenced to be crucified, but he asked to be put on the cross head downwards. He felt unworthy to die in the same way as Jesus, who had said to him long ago, 'When you were young you dressed yourself and went where you wanted to go. When you are old other hands will dress you and take you where you do not want to go.'

The sentence was carried out in Nero's circus. People say that he and Paul were both taken from prison on the same day—Paul to the milestone on the Ostian Way—Peter to Nero's circus.

When the persecution came to an end, a building, now known as the Vatican, was built over this place as a home for the Bishops of Rome. The Christians regarded themselves as a family and called the Bishop of Rome Papa, or Father, which in later years became the title 'Pope'.

So from very early days, apart from one time of exile, the Popes have lived where Peter and so many others died. It is worth remembering that the first twenty-nine Popes were all executed. Some only lasted for two months—so it was not exactly a safe job at the top. Anyone who undertook the responsibility in those years knew he was facing certain death.

The fall of Jerusalem*

ALL this time there had been increasing unrest in Jerusalem. After a while even the Roman public could not bear the cruelties of Nero any longer, and he was deposed. He killed himself to escape being killed by the men who had been his guards. In the year that followed, three other emperors were made and unmade. The man who finally took over the empire in 69 was Vespasian, who came from Britain to do so at his soldiers' insistence.

It seemed to the Jews in Jerusalem that the empire was breaking up and that they might make a bid for independence. They rose in revolt against the Romans, and succeeded at first in driving them away to the hills. But they were fighting a lost battle.

* A.D. 70.

Jesus had looked down sadly on the old city, saying, 'Oh, Jerusalem, you kill the prophets and stone those who are sent to you. I have so often longed to gather your children together as a hen gathers her chickens under her wing, but you would not come. If only you had known where your true peace lay! But you are blind. The time will come when your enemies will surround you, and bring you to the ground with all your children, and not one stone shall be left standing on another.'

And that is what happened. Another army was sent against Jerusalem, and though the inhabitants fought heroically, they could not stand up against the well armed and well trained Romans.

Titus, the son of the emperor Vespasian, said that on no account was the thousand-year-old Temple to be destroyed. It was a historic building. But the troops got out of hand. One of them tossed a burning torch into what had been known as the Holy Place, and it went up in flames.

The city was utterly destroyed, razed to the ground, as Jesus had said, and countless Jews were cruelly put to death. The Temple worship and with it the duties of the priests, whether Pharisees or Sadducees, was finished. Nor was it ever rebuilt as a Jewish Temple.

Some people, including Christians, escaped to the hills, taking some of their most precious records and documents. Perhaps they remembered what Jesus had also said, 'When you see Jerusalem surrounded by armies, then you will know that her destruction is near. Then those who are in Judæ must flee to the hills and those who are in the city must leave it, and those who are out in the country must not come in.'

So Jerusalem fell.

The Wind sweeps on

IT is hard to trace what happened in the next two or three hundred years. Some stories are known to be true. Others have been handed down by word of mouth and have become legends, but many legends and traditions are based on truth.

In some families stories are handed down from one generation to another. They may change a bit in the telling, but are basically true.

Things that happened to my great-grandmother who lived a hundred years ago, are still told in my own family. I tell them to my daughter in the words that my mother told them to me.

If you compare this with stories handed down in the first centuries after Christ you can see that a historian writing a hundred or even two hundred years later could still get hold of some accurate facts.

Of course, people improved on the stories, or forgot some part, or made mistakes, but even allowing for that, it is clear that the spark which had been blown into life at Pentecost, spread like wildfire across Europe. It also spread east to Persia and even to India.

St. Jerome, writing about the year 378, says, 'From India to Britain, all nations resound with the life and resurrection of Christ.'

A historian called Arnobius, some twenty years later, writes, 'So swiftly runs the word of God that within the space of a few years His word is concealed neither from the Indians in the East, nor from the Britons in the West.'

So bearing all this in mind we might look at the traces that are left of what happened to the other men who knew Jesus.

John is said to have gone to Ephesus. Andrew went to Greece, and he is now the Greeks' patron saint. Mark started the Church in Egypt, which is today called the Coptic Church, the old word for Egyptian. Bartholomew and Thaddeus, whose names are no more than mentioned in the Bible, are thought to have gone to Syria, and you will hear later of how their lives touched Armenia.

There is a story that Thomas went to India and died there in the year 57. Tradition links his name with what is now the State of Kerala.

One legend from very far-off days is that Joseph of Arimathea came to Britain with twelve companions. It tells how he brought with him the cup from which Jesus drank at the Last Supper, and how he founded a church at Glastonbury. This cup, the Holy Grail, was lost, and how King Arthur and his knights tried to find it many years later is another legend.

In France you find the story that Martha and Mary and Lazarus escaped from a persecution in Jerusalem and reached Marseilles. In fact the main line station from Paris to Marseilles in our own times is called St. Lazarus Station, and there is a famous church in Paris called La Madeleine or the Magdalene.

Though these stories are not history, there is nothing strange or unlikely in the underlying fact that people went enormous distances in those days with far less convenient ways of travel than we have today. You have only to look at the way Paul moved about, at the movements of the Roman soldiers, and earlier the Greeks, to realise that distance did not daunt them.

Indeed soldiers and merchants may well have been the first Christians to reach a place like Britain. This is the natural way for an idea to spread in any age. Men and women of conviction who live in practice what they believe in theory very soon pass on their ideas and their way of life. This incidentally is true of bad ideas as well as good ones, so it is important that the good ones should be lived more convincingly than the bad.

What is certain is that a great burst of new life spread out to the East and to the West. Groups of courageous men and women sprang up in many different countries. They were afraid of no one, not even of the Roman emperor, who had the power to imprison or kill them, and often did both. Men who were not prepared to sacrifice to the emperor were often blinded in one eye and lamed in one leg and then sent to work in the mines.

It is true that not everyone held out to the end. Some tried to have it both ways, and though they did not burn the incense, they paid the Roman officials to give them a certificate saying that they had. One of these has survived. It says:

TO THE COMMISSIONERS FOR SACRIFICES

IN THE VILLAGE OF ALEXANDER'S ISLAND,

FROM AURELIUS DIOGENES. . . .

AGED 72: SCAR ON RIGHT EYEBROW.

I have always sacrificed to the Gods, and now in your presence, in accordance with the law, I have done sacrifice and poured libations (offerings of drink) and tasted the sacrifices, and I request you to certify to this effect. Farewell.

Presented by me, Aurelius Diogenes.

I CERTIFY THAT I WITNESSED HIS SACRIFICE.

Aurelius Syrus.

Then, as now, there were all sorts of people in the world. But for every Aurelius Diogenes there were hundreds who held firm. They were thrown to the lions, crucified or burnt. Perhaps we lack proper records because the bodies and papers of these gallant people were destroyed with them, or else because their friends removed all traces of them for the sake of safety.

The fact that men and women and even children would rather die than say that the emperor was a god amazed all who saw them put to death, and made them want to know what power could give such strength and courage.

Though thousands died, there was no way of killing the Holy Spirit. Paul led by this Spirit had planted picked fighters all along the road to Rome in the busy cities where traders and travellers constantly met. From there they spread north, south, east and west, carrying their new faith with them.

The great business and educational centres of the Roman empire were much like what such cities are today, as far as the human nature in them was concerned. They were full of people good, bad and indifferent.

There were different races, different classes, the rulers and the ruled, the haves and the have-nots. Gradually there began to grow up cells in these places, who were in touch with God and with each other, and who began to change the whole way of life in their cities.

Through them the barriers between Jew, Greek and Roman, between Gaul and Briton, began to go down. The framework of the empire began to be the pattern of God's Plan.

It was not all going to happen at once, but here was an idea, a way of life, in which every single person, rich or poor, young or old, any race, any country, had a full part.

It was the way God planned, and still does, to bring the world into one family.

The stories that follow are not intended to be a history of the next three hundred years, but they are a pattern of the way certain men put up a fight for God's way rather than their own, and how it affected both their countries and the times in which they lived.

Polycarp*

IN the year 69 the Emperor Vespasian came to the throne, shortly after the death of Peter and of Paul. In the same year a boy was born in Asia Minor, whose name was Polycarp. Little is known of his boyhood, except that as a child he is believed to have been sold as a slave to a lady called Callisto who brought him up as her son, and left him all her money when she died.

The work done by Paul had spread from person to person throughout the province, among them the young slave and his benefactress. The apostle John, who spent the last years of his life in Ephesus, met them there.

By that time John was very old. He was the last recorded man left who had known Jesus, and he would sit for hours telling stories of the days he had spent with Him. Irenaeus, the Bishop of Lyons, in a letter written many years later, says, 'I distinctly remember the incidents of that time . . . so that I can tell you the very place where Polycarp used to sit . . . and how he would describe his talks with those who had known the Lord, and how he would relate their words.'

These talks made a deep impression on Polycarp. He gave away all the money that his former owner, the lady Callisto had left him, and devoted his life to creating the new society of which he had caught a vision from John. He became greatly loved and honoured as he grew older, and when such questions arose as, 'What did Jesus look like?', 'What did He say and do?', or 'What sort of a man was Judas Iscariot?', people would say, 'Let us go and ask Polycarp.'

All his life he travelled ceaselessly to and fro, teaching, as Ireneaus says in another letter, 'those very things which he had learnt from the apostles.'

Several emperors came and went, until in time Antoninus reigned. The terrible days of Nero were over, and Antoninus had said that the Christians were no longer to be hounded down like animals. However, there was still an order in force which said that all citizens must sacrifice to the emperor and say that he was a god.

* A.D. 69 to 155.

Antoninus wanted this done legally in front of a judge, so as to give everyone a chance of coming, as he thought, to his senses. The punishment was not always death, and there was a less cruel spirit about it as far as the emperor himself was concerned.

Unfortunately he could not be everywhere at once, and the Roman custom of having games and fights in the amphitheatres of all the great cities often brought together mobs who could not be controlled.

One day in the spring of the year 155 the proconsul Statius Quadratus was in Smyrna to represent the emperor at the games. Crowds had come from far and near. The games began with exhibitions of sword-play and gymnastics, which were only to lead up to the terrible scenes that people expected as a right, and had come to enjoy, as Paul had said in his letter to the Romans. Christians had been brought from far and near to be sure that there would be enough victims.

After the harmless opening events they were brought out. They were asked to swear that Caesar was a god, to burn incense in honour of him, and to curse Christ. But they refused, and one after another they were thrown to the lions, and killed.

The blood-thirsty crowd was delighted and called for more. Then it was that first a few, then more and more, began to call for Polycarp. He was the leader of all these Christians. He was the one who should be held responsible for all their ridiculous ideas.

Quadratus, a kindly man at heart, had no wish to have a respected old man like Polycarp killed. He had even tried to save the lives of some of the other prisoners. He was faced with a yelling mob which he could not handle, though he knew that the emperor had made it illegal for Christians to be done to death simply because the mob pressed for it.

Some Christians among the audience, who had not been discovered, slipped out quietly to warn Polycarp, who was living on a farm just outside the city. They insisted on his trying to escape. But Polycarp knew what was coming. Three days earlier, he had dreamt that there were flames all round his pillow, and he told his followers that he would be burnt to death.

Still, because they loved him, and wanted to do all they could to save him, they made him move to another house. He had only just got away when armed horsemen reached the farm looking for him. Finding only two slave boys, the soldiers tortured them until one of them gave away his master's hiding-place, and the soldiers found him.

An account written at the time has come down to us, and I will put in part of it.

'He could have got away to another farm, but would not, saying, "God's will be done." So, hearing their arrival, he came down and talked with them while all that were present marvelled at his age and constancy, and that there was so much ado about the arrest of such an old man.

'Then he ordered that something should be served for them to eat— as much as they wanted. And he besought them that they should give him an hour that he might pray freely. They gave him leave, and he stood and prayed, being so filled with the Grace of God that for two hours he could not hold his peace, while they that heard were amazed, and repented that they had come after so venerable an old man.'

However, in spite of feeling sorry, they still arrested him, and took him back to Smyrna, where he was met on the outskirts of the city by the chief of police, whose name, curiously enough, was Herod. He took Polycarp into his carriage, and reasoned with him, saying, 'Now, what harm is there in saying "Lord Caesar" and burning a bit of incense to save yourself?'

Polycarp said nothing at first, but then answered, 'I do not intend to do what you advise.'

So Herod lost patience, and decided to let him take the consequences of his obstinacy. Polycarp was turned over to Statius Quadratus, and as he walked across the great stadium a voice, which nobody could place but which the ancient records say came from heaven, called out, 'Be strong, Polycarp, and play the man.'

Quadratus wished he could get out of what he saw was coming. He knew the emperor would not approve, but he knew, too, that he was not going to be able to hold the crowd.

'Say, "Away with the atheists,"' he said, for atheist to the pagan world meant anyone who did not believe in the Roman gods. To Polycarp it meant what it means today, so he pointed at the rows of people all round the amphitheatre, and said whole-heartedly, 'Away with the atheists.'

Quadratus hoped he was beginning to see reason, and brought up the next point. 'Swear the oath and curse Christ. Then I can let you go.'

But at this the old man replied steadily, 'For eighty-six years I have served Him, and He has done me no wrong. How then can I blaspheme my King who saved me?'

Quadratus asked him once more to swear, but Polycarp replied, 'You know very well that I am a Christian, and can never say that Caesar is a god. And,' he added with spirit, 'if you would like to learn about Christianity, give me another day, and you can hear about it from me.'

'Try persuading those people,' said Quadratus, as he listened to the growing anger of the crowd, but Polycarp said he would not demean himself by arguing with them.

'I have wild beasts', said Quadratus, 'and I can throw you to them if you do not repent.'

'Send for them,' replied Polycarp. 'I cannot repent from better to worse.'

It was over. Quadratus saw that there was nothing more he could say. A herald was sent three times round the arena to announce what everybody knew already. 'Polycarp has confessed that he is a Christian.'

The ruler of the games, Philip the Asiarch (Asiarch was the title given to governors of regions in Asia), still hoped that the old man could be saved. The crowd roared, 'Bring out the lions,' but the day was drawing to an end, and Philip said that the games were over.

At this the people took the law into their own hands. They stormed over the barriers, collected wood, and seizing Polycarp they bound him to a post in the middle of the faggots. Then they lit the fire.

So the dream of the burning pillow was fulfilled, although an early story says, 'And a great flame flashed forth, and we to whom it was given to see, beheld a marvel. . . . The fire took the shape of a bellying sail, and it made a wall round the martyr's body; and there was the body in the midst, like a loaf being baked or like gold and silver being tried in the flames.'

In this account, when the flames refused to burn him, a man was ordered to kill him with a dagger. But whichever way it was, Polycarp died, and the last human link with Jesus and His times had gone. But neither the crowds there, nor history, have ever forgotten what they witnessed.

Perpetua and Felicity*

IT was not only men who decided to value God more highly than their own lives. One of the earliest stories of this choice is about a young mother called Perpetua, and her maid Felicity. They lived at Carthage in North Africa, and had heard of how two hundred years before Paul had found faith and courage through seeing Stephen die.

They knew what happened to people who said that there was a power stronger than the emperor, and were sure that if they were called upon to lay down their lives, it would convince many more. Perpetua came of a noble family, and though she was the mother of a young son, her husband does not come into the story. Either he had died, or had left her when she took this decision.

She knew what it would lead to, because the emperor, fearing the growing numbers and power of the Christians, was stamping them out as fast he could find them. In spite of this, Perpetua openly took a stand, and was arrested almost immediately.

Felicity, her maid, was also arrested and so was her teacher, Saturus, with three other men. Just before she was taken to prison, her father came and begged her to reconsider her decision. He wept. He threatened to beat her. He spoke of her baby son, but she remained quite firm.

'Father,' she said, 'do you see that jar there? Can I call it anything but a jar? I can call myself nothing but what I am, which is a Christian.'

The next day she and Felicity, with the four men, were put in prison. It was a horrible place, hot and packed with humanity, some innocent and some guilty. All were awaiting trial for crimes real or imaginary. Most of them would certainly be condemned to death. Perpetua and her friends were roughly handled by the soldiers and she suffered greatly because she had been parted from her baby.

However, two of her friends managed to have him brought to her, so she was able to feed him. She wrote in her diary, 'Immediately I gained strength, and being relieved from anxiety about my child, my

* About A.D. 180 to 203.

prison suddenly became to me a palace, so that I preferred to be there rather than anywhere else.'

She was so much at peace in her own spirit that she wrote an account of everything that happened right up to the day before she died, and the diary was carefully preserved by her family and friends, so that we can still read her words today.

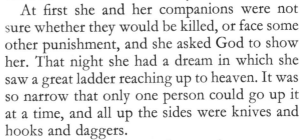

At first she and her companions were not sure whether they would be killed, or face some other punishment, and she asked God to show her. That night she had a dream in which she saw a great ladder reaching up to heaven. It was so narrow that only one person could go up it at a time, and all up the sides were knives and hooks and daggers.

In her dream Saturus, her teacher, went up first. He had voluntarily given himself up, hoping that if he admitted having taught them all, the rest of his students would be let off. When Saturus reached the top of the ladder, he turned and said, 'Perpetua, I am waiting for you. Take care the dragon does not bite you.' She looked and saw a dragon lying curled up at the foot of the ladder, so she put her foot on his head, and he drew back as if afraid of her.

When Perpetua reached the top she found a shepherd with his sheep and many others waiting to welcome her. She took this to mean that she was going on to a new life, and must prepare for it.

The day before she and her friends were to be tried her father came to see her again. He begged her not to bring sorrow and disgrace to her family. He wept and knelt before her. She too was sad to see him in such distress, but she told him gently that she was in God's hands, and must go the way He showed.

When she was questioned the next day by the judge, he asked her, 'Are you a Christian?'

'I am,' she answered. 'I cannot forsake my faith for freedom.'

Her father knew then that she would be thrown to the wild beasts, and tried to save her, but the judge only ordered him to be beaten, and this hurt Perpetua more than anything that had been done to her.

Now you may say that it was her fault that her father was hurt. She could have said she was no longer a Christian even if it was not true and it would have saved a lot of trouble. She could have gone on being one quietly without telling anyone, and everyone would have been happy.

I can only say that this does not work. Perpetua knew that lies and half-truths set no standard for anyone; that unless an idea is worth dying for, it is not worth living for: and that if enough people stood firm the idea would win through in the end.

Her maid Felicity, who was expecting a baby, prayed that it might be born before the day of execution came. God answered this prayer, and Felicity had a daughter three days before the games. Her sister took the child home and brought her up as her own.

In the arena, Saturus died first, as Perpetua had seen in her dream. Then the other men were taken. When Perpetua's turn came she went in with Felicity. A fierce cow was turned on them which tossed Perpetua in the air and wounded her, but she felt no pain and did not even know it had happened. She turned to one of the soldiers and asked when the beasts were to be let loose. She then saw that Felicity had been knocked down and went to help her up.

She stood so firm and straight and fearless that the spectators cried, 'It is enough!' She was allowed to rest for a moment, and in that time she asked to see her brother. Through him she sent a message back to her family that they must love one another, and not allow 'our suffering to keep them from the faith'.

Then she went back into the arena with Felicity. This time the order was given for them to be beheaded, which was perhaps a little less inhuman.

Many of you who read this story go into churches more or less often. Some of you go because you want to take up God's fight for the world. Others just as sightseers or to rub the brasses. Whatever you think of when you go in, it is a fact that they would never have been built unless men like Polycarp and women like Perpetua and Felicity had been ready to stake their lives on what they believed in. Many people had to die before the idea was strong enough to take root and live.

There is a saying that the blood of the martyrs was the seed of the churches. These people took God seriously, and when He said 'Give everything', they gave everything, and a fighting force was born across the world of that day.

They fought for freedom to serve God, and they won it. Today

some countries have lost that freedom because later generations took advantage of the price they paid without being prepared to pay as much themselves.

Because we have, so to speak, cashed in on the sacrifice of people braver than ourselves, we have lost a lot of territory they won. It needs courage to take God seriously even in countries where His name is written on the money, and where He is prayed to in church.

You sometimes hear people say, 'Don't talk too much about God. It may offend people who don't believe in Him.'

If Perpetua and Felicity had felt that they must not offend the non-Christians they would not have been thrown to the lions, it is true, but there would have been no Christianity either.

How am I to deal with these Christians?

ALTHOUGH terrible persecutions broke out at intervals during the next three hundred years, the Romans were not always sure what it was that they were trying to destroy. The Christians puzzled them. Their numbers were growing steadily. Though they were the most reliable and upright of all subjects, there was still something mysterious about them. The Romans felt that because the Christians stuck together and moved with a common purpose, they must be up to no good in some way.

The Romans were always afraid that any group of people who banded themselves together did so in order to overthrow the government. When the Christians refused to worship the emperor, saying that Christ was their Master, the fears of the Romans were strengthened. And yet when thousands, both rich and poor, began to join in what appeared to be an enormous secret society, it became difficult to know what to do. Surely they were not all meant to be killed.

This was expressed in some letters which passed between Pliny, the governor of the province of Bithynia, and Trajan, who was then the emperor.

Bithynia was the province to which Paul had wanted to go from Antioch in Pisidia, when he was stopped by the Holy Spirit. He was sent instead to Troas, and from there into Europe. Paul left Bithynia out of his work, yet only fifty years later Pliny says that there were so many Christians in the province that hardly anyone was buying fodder to fatten animals for sacrifice. The bottom had fallen out of the market. Town and country, city and village had taken up the new faith.

Pliny was in the habit of writing to the emperor about almost everything that came up, so as to be sure he was following the right line. On one occasion after there had been a serious fire, Pliny wrote and asked permission to start a volunteer fire brigade. But the emperor said 'No'. It was too risky to have people forming groups even for something as apparently harmless as putting out fires.

So when Pliny found that the province he had come to govern was full of Christians, he wanted to know what to do.

To make sure he wrote to the emperor saying:

'It is my rule, Sire, to refer to you in matters where I am uncertain. For who can better direct my hesitation, or instruct my ignorance? I was never present at any trial of Christians, therefore I do not know what are the customary penalties or investigations, or what limits are to be observed.'

Then he asks three questions. Are the old and the young, the strong and the weak to be given the same punishment? Should a person who decides to give up being a Christian be pardoned? Is it a crime for anyone just to say he is a Christian, if nothing else is known against him?

Pliny goes on to say, 'What I do when prisoners are brought before me, is to ask them if they are Christians. I repeat it three times, warning them that the penalty is death. If they still say "yes", I sentence them to death. Roman citizens who show the same madness I send to Rome.'

'Anyway,' he adds, 'whatever they have done they ought to be punished for their inflexible obstinacy.'

He says, rather despairingly, that dealing with these cases only produces more of them. It had also led to an anonymous pamphlet being published which gave the names of suspected Christians. Such informing, whether true or false, has always been a way of people working off grudges without getting involved themselves.

'I freed anyone,' he says, 'who on my orders did reverence to your statue with food and wine, especially when they cursed Christ, a thing which, it is said, no genuine Christian can be made to do.'

He was informed that these people made a habit of getting up very early. On certain days they met for a common meal at which they took an oath (for which the Latin word is 'sacramentum') not to be dishonest or impure. Some of them later weakened and made the sacrifice to the emperor, and the Christians who had suffered and stood firm found it hard to forgive their weaker brethren when they asked to be forgiven as soon as all danger was over.

Pliny ends by saying that this 'infectious superstition' was spreading. 'Infectious' is rather an interesting description. It meant that anyone who had it, passed it on. It was going through the cities, the villages, and the whole countryside, and had attacked people of all ages and classes.

The emperor wrote back an approving letter, saying:

'You have taken the right line, my dear Pliny, in investigating the cases of those brought before you as Christians. No hard and fast rule can be laid down. They are not to be hunted out, but they must be punished if someone informs against them and the charge is proved. But if anyone says he is not a Christian, and proves it by worshipping our gods, he shall be pardoned, however much he may have been under suspicion in the past. Pay no attention to anonymous accusations. It sets a bad example which is out of keeping with our times.'

Trajan was not a cruel man. He did not want to kill for the sake of killing. He does not seem to have been against Christianity as such, and evidently did not know what it really was. He was just against people banding together unless he knew what it was all about.

However, in spite of these instructions, thousands of men, women and children died during his reign, especially in Bithynia.

A lawyer called Tertullian writing some years later, about 197, complains of the unjust way in which the Christians were tried. He himself was one of them.

'If we really are the guiltiest of men,' he writes, 'why should we be treated differently from other criminals? The same guilt should meet with the same treatment. When others are accused on the same charges that are brought against us, they can defend themselves, or employ lawyers. They have every opportunity to reply and to ask questions, for men are not allowed to be condemned undefended and unheard.

'Christians alone are not allowed to say anything to clear themselves. . . . All that is looked for is what public hate demands, the confession of the name, not the investigation of the charge.'

These early fighters were not against authority and the law. What they were against was bribery, self-indulgence, dishonesty in themselves and others.

They were fighting for God's standards in private and in public, and it often happened that the men who judged them were not on the same side in this battle. But their idea lived on.

Origen*

FORTUNATELY certain men and their writings survived these stormy times. One of them was born about ten years after Polycarp died, and his name was Origen. He is said to have written over six thousand books in Greek and Latin, as well as letters to different people. His family lived in Alexandria and the story of his life was written by a historian called Eusebius, about a hundred years later.

Origen was the eldest of seven brothers. His father, Leonides, who was one of the revolutionary leaders of Alexandria, believed in educating his own children, and Origen learnt everything he knew from him. Leonides taught his sons that it is important to practise what you preach. Origen saw that his father lived up to his beliefs, and decided to follow his example.

This was soon put to the test, because Leonides was arrested for being a Christian. Origen would probably have been arrested too if he had gone out to try and help, but his mother hid all his clothes, so he had to stay at home. However, he wrote to his father in prison asking him not to be shaken by concern for the family.

Leonides, like so many others, stood firm and was put to death. His property was seized and his wife and children were left penniless. Origen was only seventeen, but he was not his father's son for nothing. From then on he supported his mother and brothers by teaching, which he was able to do through the training that Leonides had given him.

A wealthy lady who knew of their troubles gave him some help, so he managed to collect a library and gave lessons in literature. Leonides, as well as teaching his own family, had been the leading Christian teacher in the city, and after his death there was no one with the courage or the qualities to take it on. Origen, seeing the need, stepped into the gap. It was dangerous work, but he did it in such a way that though he was still only eighteen, the Bishop of Alexandria made him the head of the school.

This was a turning point for him. He decided to give his life to

* Born about A.D. 185, died between A.D. 251 and 254.

training people to choose God's way rather than their own. After a while he sold his books on literature, which gave him a few shillings a day to live on. He slept on the floor, and went barefoot, refusing all offers of help from his friends. Some people thought he carried his fight against self-indulgence too far, but he was waging war on softness in the nation, and never asked more of others than he did of himself.

He decided to study the Bible thoroughly, and in order to do this he learnt Hebrew, the language in which the books of what is now the Old Testament are written. Men and women flocked to his lectures because they knew they could trust him. Soon he had more to do than he could manage, and he asked Heraclas, a friend and former pupil of his, to help him.

As time went on he ran into the storms that blow around people who set new and higher standards. For one thing, having become a headmaster when he was still so young, he had no recognised training. He was not a priest (or as he would then have been called, a presbyter), but here he was giving talks on the Bible, and it worried certain people, especially the Bishop of Alexandria.

As there was so much discussion going on about him, he went away to Caesarea, where he had friends, leaving Heraclas in charge of the school. Here he went on giving talks on the Bible, and when the Bishop of Alexandria heard of it he sent for him to come back. Back in Alexandria, Origen had his lectures written down. It took seven shorthand writers to deal with all he had written. Unfortunately it led to further disapproval from the Bishop, and Origen accepted an invitation to lecture in Asia Minor, calling on his friends in Caesarea on the way.

After thinking things over he decided to be ordained as a presbyter by the Bishop there, and when he came back to Alexandria again there was another storm from the Bishop, possibly because he had not been consulted. At this point Origen seems to have felt that all these arguments were not being helpful, and he left Alexandria again, this time for good.

His going did not, however, shake people's faith in his way of teaching, and the school went on under Heraclas, and later under another old pupil, Dionysius.

Origen had interesting ideas on education. He believed that the most important part of it was to create sound and reliable people. He studied the characters of his pupils, with patient attention, we are told. He looked for what they could best do, but also saw their faults. He helped them to understand their own weaknesses, and not to be too set on their own opinions. At the same time he encouraged endurance, firmness and patience.

In his opinion, the first stage in thinking was to create the kind of character in a person which would enable him to think straight, and he tried to help his students to understand their own motives. They followed the way he showed, convinced not so much by what he said as by how he lived. He managed to make every lesson have meaning. Even in geometry and physics he showed a reason for living, because he taught people to look into everything and think it out for themselves. Man, he said, is meant to find the way to God, so he might as well begin by learning from what God has made.

After all, he argued, if you see a very fine piece of work made by a man, you want to know more about that man, how he worked and what his work was for. As you look around at all that God has made, you find yourself wanting to know more about Him, because God Himself has put into people a great longing to know why they are living, and what life is all about.

Any one person can only see part of the picture in a lifetime. But any man who in this life gets a glimpse of the riches in the mind of God, is paving the way to knowing more of them in the next.

'It is through man,' he said, 'that this world as God's work becomes perfect.'

He did not accept the excuse 'I couldn't help it.' He thought that no one need be pushed into doing anything by circumstances. A person's decision was his own responsibility, and everyone must accept responsibility for his own decisions.

He did not allow any of his ideas to be written down till he was sixty when he was really clear about what he believed and why he believed it.

Soon after this he was caught up in one of the persecutions, but though he was arrested and tortured, he was not put to death, and after a year or two he was set free. Through it all, he used his own suffering to help other people. One who was imprisoned was his old pupil Dionysius, by that time Bishop of Alexandria. Origen's letters, says the historian Eusebius, were 'full of help to those who needed encouragement'.

He had an open heart to people in need. Leaders in Church and State came to him to talk over the difficulties that confronted them, and to ask his advice.

These talks often brought unity where there had been division, and lasting answers to disputes that had seemed unanswerable.

He died about two years after his release from prison. Though he was broken in health by all that he had gone through, he was never broken in spirit, He left books of teachings which in their turn moulded the characters of great men who lived after him.

Gregory the Illuminator*

W E have come a long way from the days of the twelve apostles, but the traditions of Armenia trace this next story back to Bartholomew and Thaddeus, who are said to have gone there about the time that Paul was establishing bases in Greece and Asia Minor. Thaddeus went there, according to this account, and the first person to follow him was the daughter of the king, an eighteen-year-old girl called Sandoukht.

* Died about A.D. 336.

The Armenians were a mountain people who worshipped hard and cruel gods. But cruelty sickens people in time, and Sandoukht with many others turned thankfully to those who told them of a power stronger and yet gentler than the gods they had believed in.

When her father, the king, found he had lost his authority over her he was furious, and had her imprisoned. When not even prison could break her spirit or kill her faith, he had her tortured and killed. Thaddeus was also put to death, but it only drew more people to find out what lay behind this courage and endurance. As a result the new faith triumphed; but as the Armenians had no written language, and no means of keeping records, only stories and traditions survive from those days.

What is certain is that the way of life which was started by a few men and women lived on unrecorded. But the old ways lived on too. About two hundred years later Armenia was attacked by the King of Persia, who ordered an Armenian prince named Anak to kill the Armenian king, Khosro. Khosro, as he lay dying, gave orders that all Anak's descendants should be killed in revenge. This led to the murder of the rest of Khosro's family, and the Persians took Armenia.

Only three young children escaped the massacre of these two families. They were Gregory, the son of Anak who had killed Khosro, and Tirdat and his sister, the children of Khosro. Gregory's nurse was a Christian. We know nothing of her except that she did not panic in a crisis. Perhaps her great-grandparents had been stirred by the bravery of Princess Sandoukht. Taking Gregory with her, she escaped to Caesarea. There she brought him up in her own faith, and so kept it alive for her nation.

Tirdat was also taken to Caesarea by nobles loyal to his father, who brought him up to worship the old gods. Neither Gregory nor Tirdat knew at first that their fathers had destroyed each other. When they grew up they raised an army together. In time they reconquered their country and drove out the Persians, who during their occupation had done their best to destroy all traces of Christianity in Armenia.

Tirdat, who had become bitter as a result of his years in exile, went on with what the Persians had begun. He rebuilt the temples of the old gods and pulled down any churches that the Persians had overlooked. He reclaimed his father's throne with the help of the Roman emperor. Gregory, who had discovered the part his own father had played in the murder of Khosro, decided to serve Tirdat by way of reparation. He became his secretary.

One of the new king's first orders was that all his court should sacrifice to the goddess Anahita who, he said, had led them to victory. This Gregory refused to do. About the same time Tirdat found out that Gregory was Anak's son. So, partly because he would not stand anyone disobeying him and partly in revenge, he had him thrown into a deep pit or dungeon. Here Gregory would soon have starved to death if a woman who lived near by had not secretly thrown crusts of bread down to him every day. He remained alive for fifteen years.

During this time Tirdat went from bad to worse. A Christian girl refused to come and live with him, so he had her tortured and then killed. Gradually his conscience began to trouble him. He became ill both in body and mind, and roamed around the country almost like an animal. Though he was not an old man he seemed to be breaking up, and his sister prayed to be shown what to do. Much as she hated what he was doing, she cared deeply for him as a person. She knew what Gregory stood for, and she believed in God herself, without ever saying so publicly. As she prayed, the thought kept coming to her that she must find Gregory. This seemed nonsense, because he had been dropped into a pit fifteen years earlier and must surely be dead. However, as she could think of nothing else she went to her brother and told him that she believed their old friend was still alive.

By this time Tirdat was desperate. He was ill and wretched. Not really believing that anything would happen, he went to the underground dungeon and called his old friend's name.

You can imagine the king's amazement when he got an answer. Gregory was immediately brought out. He was terribly thin. His hair and beard had grown to an enormous length, and so had his nails, but he had a shining light in his eyes. He was neither sorry for himself nor bitter. He had spent the years in the pit praying and thinking out practical ways of helping his people if and when he was released.

Those fifteen seemingly lost years had not killed Gregory's faith, and the king asked to know more about it. Soon an amazing change took place in him, and he began to work with Gregory to let all his subjects know how to be in touch with God's Power.

The nobles and their families followed his lead, and Gregory became their friend and teacher. Groups of nobles and their families travelled

through the country teaching others. Great gifts of mind and imagination were set free, so that goods and trade began to flow where they were needed. New life came everywhere, and by the year 301 the king was able to declare Armenia to be the first country wholly under God's control.

All this went on between the years 287 and 300, while in other lands fierce persecutions were going on under the Emperor Diocletian. A flame of faith and purpose was lit by Gregory, which has made him known as Gregory the Illuminator.

King Tirdat and his people asked Gregory to become their bishop, though he was, in fact, still a soldier. Also he had a wife and two sons and might well have thought that, after being separated from them for so many years, he was entitled to go and live quietly at home. When he talked to them about it, they agreed that he should do whatever would be the most help to the country as a whole, and he went to be trained as a priest. Very soon he was made Archbishop-in-Chief, or Catholicos, of Armenia.

While Christians in others lands were being tortured and killed, the temples of the old gods were turned into churches, idols were torn down, and the cruelty and vice connected with them were brought to an end. It was done so thoroughly that to this day we know almost nothing of the Armenian religion before the time of Gregory.

One thing he did was to turn the great temple of the goddess Anahita into 'The Mother of all Christian Churches.' This goddess was supposed to be a very beautiful woman, and her followers encouraged softness and self-indulgence. Gregory brought back the idea of purity as a force in the life of the nation, so that the people

117

became strong again, and could not easily be undermined, or overrun by invaders.

His son, his grandson and his great-grandson carried on the work that Gregory started. All of them today are honoured as saints, and so are King Tirdat and his sister. They paved the way for two men a hundred years later, Mesrop and Sahag. Mesrop invented an alphabet for the Armenian language. Sahag, one of Gregory's descendants, with this alphabet, translated the Bible into Armenian. Schools and hospitals were founded, which also brought illumination to Armenia.

Armenia changed its course, and accepted God as its King and Guide. Among Armenians today there must still be the men and women who will bring illumination to their country, as Gregory did when he came out of the pit so many hundreds of years ago.

The college he founded still exists to honour the memory of what one devoted man can do for a nation, not only in his own generation, but to build the future.

The named and the unnamed

THE rushing mighty wind of truth reached out through many people, known and unknown. Polycarp in Asia Minor, Origen in Egypt, Gregory in Armenia, are among the men whose names have been handed down to us, but this tremendous outreach did not in the main come through a few outstanding people. It came through the flame of fire that burnt inside quite ordinary men and women. It seemed perfectly normal to them to listen to what Jesus told them, and obey, for they based their whole lives on the fact that Jesus was alive and at work in the world. So they passed on to others what had come to mean everything to themselves.

Some, to be sure, were people in high positions. There was a senator named Pudens who lived in Rome. You can see his house to this day. He is supposed to be the man who entertained Peter and Paul. They say he gave Peter his own chair, not so much because he wanted to, as because his little daughter Praxedes coaxed him into it. This chair is now hanging on the wall in the great cathedral of St. Peter in Rome, in the part which is built over the spot where Peter was crucified upside down in Nero's circus.

Another great man was Flavius Clemens. He was a nephew of the

Emperor Vespasian, and his wife was the emperor's niece. Flavius Clemens held the next highest post under the emperor in 95, but in 96 he was arrested and executed. His wife Domitilla was banished to a small island. You can still visit their house in Rome. There are those who think that they had a slave called Clement, who is the Clement referred to by Paul in one of his letters to Timothy, and was the third man to succeed Peter as the leader of the Christian force in Rome.

Other stories link the island of Britain with Rome, for the Romans occupied the country for over three hundred years, and for a long time were fiercely opposed by guerilla fighters. One resistance leader called Caractacus was captured and sent to Rome in the time of Paul to be in a triumphal procession for the Emperor Nero. They say his son and daughter were taken with him, and that his father, King Bran, either went with them or followed after. The story goes that they met Peter and Paul in the house of Senator Pudens.

The son and daughter became Christians, and so did Bran, who returned to Britain, full of the fire of a new idea. The old Welsh ballads tell many stories of 'Bran the Blessed'.

A Roman poet has left lines on the wedding of Pudens to Claudia, who, he says, came from 'far-off climes', 'sprung from blue-eyed Britons'. Paul, in one of his letters to Timothy, sends greetings to Pudens and Claudia, He does not say that they were husband and wife, but there is a tradition that they were and that they bought their house from Priscilla and Aquila. It became a centre of activity at the heart of the empire.

There is one nice little touch about a Roman governor of Britain who married a lady called Pomponia Graecina. Possibly she was British. She was arrested and charged with believing in a 'foreign superstition', but as her husband was the judge, he let her off.

Later on a Welsh chief named Lleurwg is said to have written to Rome for teachers to come and train his people in the new faith. There is a church in the city of London called St. Peter's-upon-Cornhill, in which is a tablet saying that it was founded by Lleurwg, or Lucius, to give him his romanised name. Legends in Wales tell of his being the great-great-grandson of King Bran.

One could spend a long time sorting out all these stories, and trying to decide if they are true, but a wise old man called Fuller, writing in 1648, says that it does not really matter. He says that churches always want to claim some apostle as their founder, in case people should think less well of them for having been started by any 'inferior preacher'. This, he thinks, is rather like the way pagan people feel they must claim their descent from a god, and it may be that the very fact that we do not know is part of God's plan. It was His work anyway.

'We see the light of the world shined here,' writes Fuller, 'but see not who kindled it.'

This seems to be good sense. The point is not who started it hundreds of years ago, but whether we live it now. The Holy Spirit lived on through thousands of men and women whose names we shall never know, but they made history. History may not know our names either, but we can make it just as they did.

The Romans never conquered the whole of Britain, but having mastered the southern part they shut off the rest by a wall, the remains of which are still standing. This wall was to keep out two savage tribes: the Scots from Ireland, who finally settled in the north and gave their name to Scotland; and the Picts from Scandinavia. At intervals these tribes came swarming over the wall, killing and burning everything in their path. The Britons clung to the Romans for protection, and many of them did not feel like antagonising the only people who seemed to them to be able to save them from the invaders.

This made the flame of faith burn low for a while. The Britons did not see the point of being saved from the Picts and the Scots only to be killed by the Romans for being Christians.

However, little fires of faith did remain alight and grow stronger. People whose names are unknown held on, until once again they became a force strong enough to be reckoned with. The result was that when in 303 the Emperor Diocletian set on foot the tenth and last great persecution, there were in Britain some Christians to persecute.

The first who is recorded to have been put to death was a man called Alban. He was a soldier. He admired the Christians, without being one of them, until one day a priest, who was being hunted by the Romans, came to him for shelter. Alban was so impressed by the quality of this man that he determined to save him, and when soldiers came to search the house, he put on the priest's clothes and had himself arrested instead. One story has it that the priest was also a prince, the son of King Lucius who had sent for teachers from Rome. Whoever he was, Alban let him escape.

Alban was then brought before the judge and told to sacrifice to the emperor. He refused, saying that he was now a Christian, so he was condemned to be beheaded.

The soldier who was ordered to carry out the execution was so stirred by Alban's courage that he refused to do it, and was beheaded too. This happened in a town then known as Verulamium, but later renamed St. Albans in honour of the first martyr in the island of Britain.

On the whole, though, the persecution in Britain was not so severe as in some other countries. The Roman governor at the time of St. Alban did not have his heart in slaughtering men and women because of what they believed.

One day he gave an order that all his court should come and burn incense to the emperor. Everyone knew that death was officially the punishment for those who refused, so when the moment came, some who were known as Christians weakened. They threw incense into the fire, saying, as they had been told to do, that the emperor was a god.

The rest of the Christian courtiers firmly refused.

The governor stood watching, and when everyone had chosen one way or the other, he said to those who had tried to play safe, 'People who are false to their God will never be true to their prince,' and dismissed them from their posts.

To the others he gave greater responsibility because he knew he could trust them.

The governor's name was Constantius Chlorus, and the next story is about his son, whose name is now known to history as Constantine the Great.

The Emperor Constantine*

CONSTANTINE was an unusual character. His father was a Roman general and administrator. His mother, according to some, was the daughter of a British chief, possibly the one whose name has survived as Old King Cole. Others say she came from Asia Minor. She is now known as Saint Helena.

Her son Constantine was no saint, but he was a man of vision. Without him we should never have had Europe as we know it today.

He was born as the Roman empire was moving towards its fall. It had become too unwieldy to be governed by one man, and the Emperor Diocletian had divided it into two. There was a western empire and an eastern empire, each ruled by an emperor with the title of Augustus. Each emperor had under him a second-in-command called the Caesar. Diocletian's plan was that the two emperors would reign jointly for twenty years, after which they would retire together leaving the caesars to succeed them.

The caesars were not to be their sons, in order to avoid getting the power into the hands of any one family. It was a good idea in theory, but not so easy to work out in practice.

Constantius, the father of Constantine, was the western caesar, and when Diocletian the western emperor retired according to plan in the year 305, Constantius moved into his place. The emperor of the east rather unwillingly retired too and was succeeded by his caesar, Galerius. So far so good, but complications soon set in.

The new eastern emperor Galerius had a son-in-law called Maxentius who had now become the western caesar, and Galerius wanted to be sure that this son-in-law would move up to become the western emperor.

One possible block to the plan was young Constantine, who was being educated at the court of Galerius in the east. If he should decide to try and succeed his father, it would spoil Maxentius' chance of becoming emperor. Galerius accordingly kept Constantine so closely guarded on the pretext of looking after him, that he was practically a prisoner.

* A.D. 307 to 337.

When he was about eighteen, Constantine realised this and decided to escape. He managed to get away with all the post horses to stop anyone from coming after him. Then he headed for the west, with all possible speed, to join his father.

Constantius was delighted to see his son. He had been partly in Gaul and partly in Britain, and was about to sail from Gaul to put down a rising of the Picts in the north of Britain. Constantine arrived just in time to go too. Father and son marched north together, but when they reached York the father fell ill and died. Constantius had been much loved by his men, and during the long march they had come to know and respect his son, so the soldiers immediately elected Constantine to succeed him.

This was exactly what Diocletian had hoped would not happen. Galerius, the eastern emperor, had also hoped it would not happen because it upset his plans for Maxentius, who now regarded himself as the western emperor.

Constantine tactfully said he would be the Caesar for the time being, and wrote to Galerius telling him so. He had the army behind him and Galerius saw he could do nothing to prevent it.

This was only the beginning of a long struggle in which six men, most of them related by marriage to one or more of the others, claimed the title of emperor.

After a while Maxentius, who had established himself in Rome, persuaded the retired eastern emperor to join a plot against Constantine. Constantine decided that this was going too far, and marched on Rome to recapture it.

On the way there he had an experience which proved to be a turning point in the history of Europe and indeed of the world. Many years later he told the historian Eusebius about it.

He was in camp, he said, with his army just outside Rome, when he saw in the sky a flaming cross and written round it were the words, 'By this sign conquer'.

It made him think. The Cross was not a new idea to Constantine. His father had respected the men and women who based their lives on the teaching that God's will must cross man's will. They were known and respected by many, if not by all, and Constantine must have become convinced that what they stood for was true. He had not stood for it himself, but when he saw the sign and the message, he believed he was meant to act on it.

He gave orders for a banner to be made bearing this sign, and at

Milvian Bridge, with the banner at the head of his army, moved into
battle. There he defeated his rival Maxentius in the year 312.

Constantine was first and foremost a soldier. Nobody could have
called him a saintly man, but winning a battle was something he could
understand. It could also mean that the Cross of Christ was meant to
win, and that the men and women who put it first in their lives were
not meant to be destroyed.

He was now undisputed ruler of the west. His old rival Galerius had died the year before, which had resulted in two men, Licinius and Maximin, fighting each other for the title of emperor. Licinius, who had married Constantine's sister, won this struggle, and during a brief period of peace between the brothers-in-law, they signed an order that the persecution of Christians was to come to an end.

However, this did not last long. War broke out between them which ended in the defeat of Licinius, and for the first time for many years the empire was united under one man. There were, though, still two capitals—one in the west at Rome—and the other in the east at Byzantium, now called Istanbul.

Rome had become more and more the home of every kind of evil. Money, laziness and cruelty ruled men's lives. Her leaders, like those of Jerusalem, had turned away from the life which men like Peter and Paul offered them.

It seemed to Constantine that there needed to be a new Rome. He decided to make a fresh start and chose Byzantium as his capital. He had it rebuilt and renamed it Constantinople after himself. In less than six years a great new city with palaces and churches had risen on the rocks by the Black Sea.

Here Christianity became the official religion of the empire. Other rulers had tried unsuccessfully to stamp it out, but Constantine had seen in his own mother and in the other people who followed Christ, certain qualities which his empire needed.

He could see that if these qualities of faithfulness, honesty, purity and unselfishness could be built into the newly reborn empire, they would forge strength, and above all unity.

So people who had met in secret and had often had to go into hiding, came into the open. Men who had once been hounded down were given responsible positions in the government. Slavery and many forms of cruelty began to die out. The empire became officially a Christian state.

This was a great step forward. On the other hand, once it was no longer a struggle for survival life became easier for the former revolutionaries.

The emperor approved. The neighbours approved. People no longer felt the need to stick together.

Arguments and differences of opinion grew between one group and another. Disagreements arose about what God was like and about what sort of person Jesus really was.

Looking around him Constantine saw the people on whom he had relied, hopelessly divided. His dream of a united Christian empire showed signs of falling to pieces before it had started. He knew that without a common aim and faith, it would certainly collapse.

So in 325 he gathered the Christian leaders together to talk things over. They met in the town of Nicea, in Bithynia.

Many of the men he summoned had been through persecutions under earlier emperors. Some had been partly lamed and blinded. Most of them had suffered in some way or another because of what they believed. They were survivors of a gallant band, and were received with honour by a guard of soldiers who might well, a few years earlier, have put them to death.

At this gathering, which is known as the Council of Nicea, they reached agreement on what they believed and wrote it down. It was called a 'Creed' from the Latin 'Credo' meaning 'I believe'.

This agreement was called the Nicene Creed and it is interesting that it was the rough half-pagan soldier Constantine who saw the need

for agreement and took steps to find it. One historian, Stanley, said that he was called Great more for what he did than for what he was, because he saw the future which lay before Christianity and decided to enlist it in the service of his empire.

Constantine was not a dedicated character like Paul and others of whom you have heard. He almost certainly ordered the death of his wife and eldest son, yet he opened the doors of the empire to the idea that there was a great uniting plan for nations. He was feeling after something and he acted on what he saw as far as he saw it. He created a framework in which people could at any rate begin to work it out, and from this grew the conception of what came to be known as Christendom.

A Stronghold established

FROM a hundred and twenty men and women in one room to the bounds of the known world. That is the story of the first three hundred years of the Age of the Holy Spirit, which is the age we are still in.

'But', you may say, 'I don't see much sign of the Holy Spirit. So many terrible things are happening in the world. Perhaps the age of the Holy Spirit was just a short period, which is now over.'

Not at all. It was the beginning of a new stage in God's continuing and unfolding plan to win the world. It was not that people became perfect, but that they took up the fight. It was not that difficulties and suffering came to an end, but that courageous men and women found how to overcome them through a Force sent into the world by God for that very purpose.

Human nature being what it is, there are always those who would like to play safe and sit down somewhere behind the lines. They think that they could then live in peace, and not get involved in anything uncomfortable. We are not talking about them. The people whose stories you have read had no such idea. It is true that if they had kept quiet about what they stood for they would not have been thrown to the lions. They would not have risked their jobs, their reputations, their popularity and their lives. They would have lived and died, perhaps uneventfully, and we should never have heard of them again.

On the other hand we should never have heard, either, of the Way of living which Jesus died to show. History, as we now know it, would never have happened. As it was, those first three hundred years were shaped by men and women who were so intent on passing on their faith to others that they had no time or opportunity to write the history they were making with their lives. They could not stop and write memoirs. Being persecuted was about the only opportunity they had for witnessing in public, and the best of them rejoiced when they found they were going to die for their Master in front of anything up to eighty thousand people. The emperor and empress were often among the onlookers.

In these great amphitheatres, something like the football stadiums of today, they took the opportunity to show what they believed. They proclaimed their faith, and their certainty of its victory in this world and the next. Everyone else thought that death was the final disaster, but the people we now call martyrs knew it was not.

'Martyr' is simply the Greek word for 'witness', and they were witnesses to something they knew was true. The result was that in course of time they won through, and established the fact that God rules in the affairs of men.

By the year 330, when Constantine proclaimed Christianity as the official faith of the empire, they had created a tremendous network which stretched from Britain to the Persian border and across it into India and China. Cells of new life sprang up everywhere which in turn produced others. The empire itself, however, was already moving to its fall. Less than a hundred years later Rome fell, overwhelmed by war-like tribes from the east, but the net was so strong that in the end it caught and held them too.

The battle went on, and still does. Of course there have been ups and downs, divisions and disasters, victory and defeat, but that is what one expects in warfare. Every child who is born comes into this fight and has to choose on which side to enlist, and there is no retiring age and no pension. There is no settling down to a life where God hands out ice-cream, and everything goes smoothly.

If that is what you want, there is no point in reading the next part of this book.

If, however, you want to know how men and women have fought for God's Plan down the years, how they changed the history of nations, and how the fight goes on today, there is more to come.